Carl Sampson

D&B PUBLISHING

www.dandbpublishing.com

First published in 2008 by D&B Publishing

Copyright © 2008 Carl Sampson

British Library Cataloguing-in-Publication Data

A catalogue record for this book is available from the British Library.

ISBN 987-1-904468-38-7

All sales enquiries should be directed to D&B Publishing:

Tel: 01273 711443, e-mail: info@dandbpoker.com,

Website: www.dandbpoker.com

Carl Sampson can be contacted at Carl@Pokerquest.f9.co.uk

Cover design by Horatio Monteverde.

Printed and bound in the UK by Clays, Bungay, Suffolk.

CONTENTS

About the Author

Carl Sampson first started out in the gaming industry in very modest surroundings. He worked as a croupier and later as a gaming inspector in numerous casinos across England. He was far from happy with his job and the lack of promotional opportunities certainly didn't help. Despite the fact that Carl disliked his job and many of the people whom he had to deal with daily, he was highly captivated by the inner workings of his profession.

Unknown to his employers, Carl set about learning and investigating the weaknesses of casino games and being an employee on the inside afforded him access to information that other people didn't have. The pay at that time was poor compared with other professions, but Carl was secretly accumulating knowledge – a vast amount of knowledge.

Carl left the gaming industry for good in 1998 and worked as a financial consultant for a few months, but his heart was not in it. However, while he was on a company induction course in Bournemouth he became acquainted with someone who was later to become his financial backer for a highly successful blackjack team that Carl ran between 1998 and 2002.

This was Carl's first venture into the world of professional gambling and, despite a rocky initial period, his team was responsible for winning very large sums of money both in England and Europe. While Carl was involved with his first blackjack team, he also got involved for the first time with roulette and professional roulette teams.

People were coming from all over the country to pick Carl's brains to find out what he knew about roulette. Carl's blackjack team finally broke up in 2002 and shortly afterwards Carl took up playing poker professionally on the internet. He had been a keen student of poker for many years and had done very well in cash games, but online poker gave him the opportunity to continue his career as a professional gambler. Carl came by his nickname "The Dean" when playing in a local poker game. Whenever someone wanted to know the odds of hitting a certain hand, Carl was always there with the answer and they started to call him "The Dean of Poker", which was later shortened to "The Dean".

Carl has done very well playing in middle limit Texas hold'em cash games and has recently switched to playing no limit hold'em cash games. Early in 2005, Carl began writing for four poker magazines, *Poker Pro Europe*, *Bluff Europe*, *Online Poker Pro* and the official magazine of the televised, *World Poker Tour*.

Carl has also written another very successful book, *Princes of Darkness: The World of Highstakes Blackjack*, which tells the true account of Carl's team.

Carl works as a gambling consultant for several websites and has consulted casinos on advantage play and cheating He also acted as a consultant with an international film company in 2003 on cheating inside casinos. These days Carl can be found crushing online cash games, which he still plays regularly, and on his website (www.pokersharkpool.com), where he talks about all things poker. On his site he also offers coaching and advice on poker.

INTRODUCTION

So you thought that roulette couldn't be beaten? Well you are far from being on your own because the overwhelming majority of people think this as well. On the evolutionary ladder of roulette knowledge, you start off with the punters at the bottom who think that they have come up with some foolproof system to beat the game and that they are in possession of knowledge that no one else has. To put it crudely, these people are suffering from delusion and deserve everything that they get. The term "a fool and his money are soon parted" springs to mind.

If I'm being overly critical of these people then forgive me, but I had to endure their crap for nearly ten years so I'm sure that you will excuse my low opinion of these people coupled with the odd rant. Armed with what little they know, how on earth they can believe that they can overcome a professional industry, or that they have discovered a holy grail that has eluded some of the greatest mathematicians on the planet over the past several hundred years, is beyond me.

Then we start to move on from the deluded system players to the people who know better. They understand that the house has an undisputed edge and that the structure of the game forbids it from being beaten by any gambling system. They know that the casino offers odds that are in their favour and that this edge will eventually defeat even the luckiest of punters. These people are in the overwhelming majority and either never play roulette or they fully understand that they can't beat it and only play the game recreationally.

Then you come to the very tiny percentage of people who know and understand about the game's weaknesses and just how they can be overcome. These people tend to be the gaming managers or higher up the casino chain of command. This is the kind of knowledge that does not filter down to the shop floor gaming staff, who are told strictly only what they need to know and they *don't need to know!*

The turnover of staff in casinos is fairly large, so dealers and inspectors are only told what they need to know to be able to do their job to the fullest without it jeopardising the security of the casino. Your average croupier, inspector or pit boss for that matter will be totally unaware of most of the information given in this book.

In fact the overwhelming majority of gaming managers will be unaware of what is in this book because there are certain skills like spinning sections and spinning out of sections for instance that many people feel just cannot be accomplished. Having the ability to spin sections has been derided in numerous quarters as being impossible. People quote parrot fashion what they have heard or been told regarding the high-quality John Huxley wheels being totally random… utter rubbish!

There is no such thing as a totally random wheel, but the skill of spinning in and out of certain sections can also be achieved *if* the dealer is skilled enough – few are. It is those same 35 to 1 paybacks that are the Achilles' heel in roulette. The house advantage on single zero roulette as it is played in England is 2.7 per cent. If you were to play even chances, where you would receive half of your wager back should zero come, this advantage would be cut in half to a mere 1.35 per cent.

This is enough to grind down the system players, but those kind of tiny percentages leave the game vulnerable when attacked from other directions. The paranoia regarding roulette on behalf of the casino hierarchy can be demonstrated by the fact that many of them routinely alternate the wheels after closing time. Why do they do this? Read on and you will discover why – it sure isn't to even out the wear and tear like they tell the staff.

Looking back at my career in the gaming industry, it is clear that I missed a very serious opportunity. I could easily spin out of certain sections when I had my wheel travelling at a certain speed and there were several other members of staff who could do the same.

I could have won the casino a lot of money had I give a damn, but that would have been a total waste anyway. The true advantage lies in working in collusion with a punter and I knew certain dealers who were in fact doing this. CCTV inside a casino is more a deterrent for the staff than the punters, but few people realise that.

But you certainly don't have to be a dealer or to have worked inside a casino to have understood the mysteries of the spin. There were several punters down the years who always beat us by reading the spin and the wheel. How did they do this? Read on and you will find out. You will also discover how clued-up roulette players have been destroying this game long before you or I were even born.

In this book you will also learn how biased wheels are formed and how to detect them as well as how professionals cheat on roulette. You may ask me why I have written this book when it will educate the very people who have been a serious revenue source for me down the years. I must confess to doing it for egotistical reasons, but in any case they are powerless to stop some of the tactics that we still employ.

The latest team that I trained won over £50,000 in a six-month period in 2005–2006, without the merest hint of being detected. In this book you will learn about methods and techniques that the entire gaming industry does not want you to know. Interspersed in *Killer Roulette* are true accounts of events that happened to real people in England between 2000 and 2006.

All of these people have one very important thing in common: a desire to find out the truth about the game that many people think cannot be beaten. So read on and be prepared to be amazed. As the great Albert Einstein once said: "Imagination is much more important than knowledge; knowledge is limited whereas imagination encircles the world." To that profound statement by the great physicist I add this: anything that's created or invented by man can be overcome by man... and that certainly includes roulette!

Carl "The Dean" Sampson,

September 2008

CHAPTER 1

OUR ROULETTE ANCESTORS... MY HEROES!

Over the past one hundred years or so, there have been certain individuals who have won huge amounts of money on roulette... and not by chance, either! The characters you will read about are *real* people and not fictitious figure in a movie. The reason why I have included them in this book is mainly because I wanted you to be aware of them, and to make you realise that what I'm saying is true, because what these people did and the amounts they won have been documented.

If there was ever to be a roulette roll of honour then every single one of these talented and knowledgeable individuals would be on it and I salute them all because they were my inspiration.

The American Adventurer

In the last few years of the nineteenth century, a young man graduated from the University of Illinois by the name of William Nelson Darnborough, who would eventually go down into roulette folklore. Darnborough drifted from job to job after leaving university but one thing remained... his intense fascination with roulette.

What attracted William to the game or fascinated him so greatly isn't known, but we do know that he purchased his very own roulette wheel and studied the mechanics of it and its motion for considerable lengths of time. He travelled across America taking on all comers, winning considerable amounts of money from drifters and losing gamblers.

But the event that was to catapult Darnborough into the public eye was to happen in Monte Carlo in 1904, when Darnborough was in his mid-30s. He won a reported £83,000 playing roulette, which for that era was a staggering amount of money. There are accounts on record that were recorded by eye witnesses who were there.

All of them report that Darnborough moved with alarming speed when placing his bets and that he only started to place his bets after the dealer had spun the ball. What makes this event all the more remarkable was that Darnborough was far from being a one-hit wonder and continued to hit the casinos very hard for a good number of years.

It is also reported that Darnborough didn't play the same numbers from spin to spin, which totally rules out that he may be playing lucky numbers or that he may have detected a biased wheel. At his peak Darnborough was reported to have won in the region of half a million dollars from the casinos in Monte Carlo, a figure that would be the equivalent of tens of millions in today's money.

I would have loved to have been there in person and watched the man in action – it seems ludicrous to me to try and explain his success away as just one of those things. There is absolutely no doubt in my mind that Darnborough was perhaps the first recorded case of a punter actually reading the spin. This was easier to do in the old days with the design of the wheels at that time. They nearly all had deeper slots, which meant that wherever a ball dropped, it tended to stay in that general area.

Darnborough was at it again in Monte Carlo in 1911, where he once again won a "very considerable sum of money". The event that seemed to end Darnborough's run was not anything done by the casino or the fact that he lost it back. He met and married an English girl named Frances, who loathed gambling and she made William promise never to go back to that life ever again despite his success. Darnborough died in 1958 aged 90, never once telling anyone about just how he had managed to win the money that had made him so rich.

I've read several reports from individuals who have claimed that Darnborough couldn't possibly have been reading the spin because this is far too difficult a task. They are half right in the fact that it is a very difficult task; if it was easy then everyone would be doing it and the entire world would be populated by computerised mechanical roulette wheels.

But these people are wrong because it can be done even on the modern wheels. The technique of exactly how to do it finally hit me after a very considerable length of time practising it on a real roulette wheel. People who have no experience of working in the casino industry wouldn't know what I was talking about, in fact the overwhelming majority of people who *do* work in the casino industry wouldn't know what I was talking about.

Let me put something to you. Let's say that you wanted to play professional poker and you asked one hundred regular poker players how well they were doing. If all of them told you the truth, which was that not a single one of them was making the game pay, would you then conclude that it wasn't possible to play poker for a living? Many people would reach this conclusion but they would be completely wrong.

Let me put something else to you, which may make any sceptic see what I'm trying to say. The house edge on single zero roulette is 2.7 per cent. If you were to place one chip on all 37 numbers (1–36 plus zero) then you would lose exactly one chip because your winning number would pay 35 to 1 plus your bet back, so you would return 36 chips. What this means is that if we take the figure of 100 per cent and divide it by the amount of numbers in the wheel, then we get a figure of 2.7 per cent per number.

It is now very easy to see how this method could work, because if you could reach a stage where you could eliminate just two numbers in the wheel from winning, then that 2.7 per cent house edge would be transferred to the player, and that's huge in gambling terms. Any professional card counter would give their high teeth for that kind of edge.

This is why the exponents of those who think it can't be done have seriously got it wrong. You don't need to be able to spin certain numbers or certain blocks, for that matter; in fact you don't have to be able to hit anything. All you need to know is that just two numbers will not be hit during the course of this spin. Do you still think that it is impossible now?

Darnborough had worked this out – or his accomplice had, which has been reported in some sources. Of course it is perfectly feasible that this wasn't Darnborough's idea, but someone else's, someone who simply didn't have the money to hit the tables as hard as Darnborough, although this explanation seems unlikely to me. The people on the inside know what Darnborough was doing even a century later. To be able to do this at all you must first believe that it can be done. The people who still refuse to believe that a punter can read a spin after reading about William Nelson Darnborough are ignoring the obvious.

The Used Car Salesman

We fast forward now to 1986 to hear about the incredible story of Billy Walters. He was a used-car salesman and a known big hitter in Las Vegas who regularly won and lost huge amounts of money. But in 1986 Billy Walters hit the casinos in Atlantic City on roulette in a big way. Only this time he was doing something different... a lot different.

What Billy Walters did was to make a proposition never seen or heard before in Atlantic City. He offered to deposit a sum believed to be $2 million with a casino in return for them increasing their maximum wagers on roulette. A casino called the Golden Nugget accepted the offer and Billy flew in from Las Vegas to start his date with destiny.

This is where Walters' methods varied drastically from Darnborough's: he bet $2,000 per number on five numbers and never once varied his bet. What initially struck the casino staff as being odd was that Walters insisted on playing on double zero roulette instead of single zero. It is here where the edge for the house dramatically increases to a whopping 5.26 per cent.

Instead of fearing that they were being set up, the casino gaming staff just took Walters as another impulsive gambler who didn't have a clue about what he was doing. After all they knew full well about his reputation for losing big sums of money in Las Vegas, which meant that they were more than happy to accommodate him.

Walters played five numbers – 7, 10, 20, 27 and 36. For the benefit of European readers, 7 and 20 and 10 and 27 are situated next to each other on a double zero American wheel. Walters and an associate of his played for hour after hour and it was soon evident to all present that the casino management was worried.

A procession of worried telephone calls and huddled meet-
ings told everyone that the big chiefs at the Golden Nugget were
far from happy. On and on, Walters relentlessly played the same
numbers. Sometimes he would go for a break and his associate
would hold the fort and continue the action. Every time that
Walters hit one of his five numbers, the payout was $70,000 less
the $8,000 that he lost on the other four numbers, leaving him
with a win of $62,000.

With action totalling $10,000 per spin, Walter's actual expec-
tation per spin was minus $526 so it was no wonder that the ca-
sino welcomed his action at the outset. But after almost forty
hours of continual play, and Walters being $4 million ahead, the
casino bigwigs terminated the game. They also tried to circulate
stories in the local newspapers that Walters had just gotten
lucky. The truth was that this wasn't down to luck and the casino management knew it.

Suddenly they understood why Walters had not played on
the much better single zero wheels. It wasn't because he was a
dummy but because there was something wrong with the wheel
that he had been playing on. Billy Walters was ruthlessly exploiting what is known as a biased wheel, and he was exploiting
it to the full.

A biased wheel is one where the near randomness of the outcome has been interrupted, for whatever reason. This can be
done artificially by an individual but most of the time it is
caused by constant repetitive wear and tear. But the misinfor-
mation that was put out by the casino bosses was just another
example of them not wanting the truth to be known.

Even the best roulette wheels in the world, like John Huxley,
are subject to wear and tear. It is just that certain types of wheels
are more susceptible to going wrong than others. The Huxley
wheels are without doubt the Rolls-Royces of the roulette wheel

industry but even Rolls-Royces break down if they are used often enough.

So why did the casino stand for Walters' action for so long before calling time? Well, first, no one had ever been hit to that scale before with biased wheel play. Second, Walters' history as being a known big hitter and a losing gambler to boot gave him the perfect cover for his coup. When it became apparent what was happening it was too late. But when a punter like Billy Walters asks to deposit $2 million with you and he gets ahead by $500,000, do you really want to risk offending him, when you perceive that he will lose it all back and the $2 million on top?

As it later turned out, Walters had a team of wheel clockers touring the casinos in Atlantic City doing nothing else but taking down numbers. He already had the data at his disposal and all he needed to know was how to interpret it correctly to see if a bias existed. This process of identifying real bias and not imaginary patterns is an area that's not well understood by many casino managers and certainly not back in the mid-1980s. This is an area that I've worked on over many years and I pass on the information to any team that's interested in attacking roulette in this way.

Mathematicians have calculated that the probability that Walters' win was purely down to luck as being in the region of 2 per cent, which when converted to odds is 49 to 1. When you couple this statistic with the story about the teams of wheel clockers then you can't dismiss this as chance.

The English Engineer

If you thought that detecting biased wheels was a new concept then think again. A Yorkshireman by the name of Joseph Jaggers arrived in Monte Carlo in 1873. Like Darnborough, Jaggers was intensely fascinated by the game of roulette. What Jaggers failed to accept was the belief that roulette couldn't be beaten and that the roulette wheels produced totally random results. Jaggers for me was the real hero in the roulette roll of honour because it was he who first questioned the widely accepted belief that roulette was unbeatable except by cheating methods.

Biased wheels are like an itch that the casinos cannot scratch, and despite all the hype about the current crop of wheels, it isn't going to go away. What was remarkable about Jaggers was that unlike the vast majority of punters, who have won big amounts of money on roulette, he had never set foot inside a casino before to anyone's knowledge, and he didn't even know the intricacies of the game or the dealing procedures.

Just like Billy Walters over a hundred years later, Jaggers had a team of wheel clockers working for several days doing nothing but taking down numbers. Nothing like this had ever been seen before by the casino, so they allowed it to happen without so much as a second thought. When Jaggers finally took it upon himself to enter the casino, he did so armed with the knowledge that one of the wheels was exhibiting a strong bias towards certain numbers.

By the end of the day, Jaggers was ahead by $70,000. As he left, the casino could be forgiven for thinking that this was the last that they would see of this mysterious Englishman and that their worries were over… They were wrong! Jaggers returned the following day and proceeded to bet on the same numbers as he had bet the previous day, and once again won more money. Jaggers had losing spells but his winnings slowly but surely escalated during the day. The funny thing about this story was that the gaming action in the rest of the club almost ground to a halt while Jaggers was in action.

Jaggers was ahead by about $300,000 by the end of the day

and, to cap it all off, the casino had suffered substantial extra losses by other punters blindly following his numbers and backing them themselves. What followed was perhaps the first ever serious casino counter measure to deal with a biased wheel player. After the casino had closed, the staff clandestinely switched the wheels around because by this time they did suspect that something may be wrong with the wheel.

Jaggers came back to the casino again the following day and failed to notice the switch. He had lost $150,000 of his winnings back to the casino before he realised that something was not right. He had noticed certain marks in the grain of the wood on the wheel where he had been so successful and went searching for the wheel inside the casino... he found it!

Jaggers ramped up his winnings on this wheel to roughly $500,000. But by this time the casino bosses had figured out the likely cause of the biased wheel. They thought that the fault lay in the frets (dividers that separate the numbers) and decided to thwart Jaggers by replacing them after-hours. Jaggers must surely have known or at least suspected that the casino wouldn't stand for such large losses. Once he knew that they were on to him when they changed the wheels around, he must have known that it was a matter of time before his run ended because the casino would simply have ended it for him by forcing him to stop, or by simply taking that particular wheel out of action.

The next day with the problem of the frets seemingly solved, the casino opened their doors to Joseph Jaggers once again. He proceeded to lose heavily and his winnings tumbled down to about $300,000. At this stage Jaggers did the smart thing and quit, and he lived the rest of his natural life an incredibly wealthy man. Even today I still drink a toast to Joseph Jaggers from time to time.

The Rashid Khan syndicate

What made the Rashid Khan syndicate so remarkable was that this was perhaps *the* greatest bias wheel coup of them all. It wasn't the greatest amount of money won, nor was it the most famous, but in my opinion what makes this pretty damn good is because some of the wheels that they were going up against were the modern, low-profile, high-quality wheels made by John Huxley.

The amount won was in the region of £150,000 in 2003 and 2004; three of the casinos involved were in the south of England. For obvious reasons, the names of the casinos where these amounts were won must remain a secret but that's quite common with successful wheel players. It is the smaller amounts of money that the grassroots players win that go unnoticed. When a 25p colour chip player gets a good grasp of just how to beat a dealer then when they win a couple of hundred quid, no one gives a damn.

Finding biased wheels is a much more difficult task these days because the Huxley wheels are made by top quality craftsmen. They are engineered to tight tolerances yet they still have weaknesses, even now. The modern low profile wheels were invented to wipe out biased wheel play and to a large extent they did, but not completely. What the casino bosses don't really seem to take on board fully, in my opinion, is that there are large numbers of people with nothing better to do than figure out ways to extract money from gambling establishments, and these people are not dummies.

London is a prime target for roulette teams because there are many casinos, so there are many roulette wheels in a rather small area and the maximums are much greater. Rashid Khan was a Pakistani businessman based in Sutton Coldfield. What his line of business was I'm not prepared to divulge but he came to me in the summer of 2003 to seek my advice on roulette. He and three business colleagues were willing to put a very substantial bankroll together to hit roulette if they could encounter a biased wheel.

They basically wanted to know how to detect a biased wheel and where they were likely to find one. After listening to what I had to say, and seeing the data that I provided them with, they initially took their knowledge into Europe where they won just over $20,000 in an unlicensed casino in Holland, beating a biased wheel there.

Rashid Khan had business associates and contacts all over western Europe and won further amounts of £12,000 and £15,000 on biased wheels in France and Germany. He came back to England in 2004 and immediately took £27,000 from another casino in London. But that same year Rashid got wind of a biased wheel in two casinos in the south of England and took those casinos for £40,000 over the course of eighteen months, before the wheels were removed.

He used accomplices to place the bets so that no one person was responsible for winning large amounts of money. Whether the casinos cottoned on isn't known to me, but the fact was that those two wheels were never seen again by Rashid or any of his accomplices.

So much for the indestructible John Huxley wheels: magnificent creations they may be but they are not made of kryptonite and will be subject to wear and tear just like anything else. But the things are so damned expensive to replace that most casinos don't bother. They know full well that the overwhelming majority of punters don't have enough information to beat them, even if they do happen to run across one that's faulty. So they keep the same wheels for too long and don't carry out adequate servicing procedures most of the time. When I worked in the industry, they didn't even properly level the damn things before the start of a shift. They used a bog standard spirit level at the beginning of the day and that was it.

Getting back to our friend Mr Khan, he won in the region of £150,000 from roulette and returned to his native Pakistan in the winter of 2005. His accomplices remain in the country and are public enemy number one in England... if the gaming industry knew who they were that is!

The Eudaemons

In 1985 Thomas A. Bass wrote *The Eudaemonic Pie*, later renamed *The Newtonian Casino*, which went into great detail about plans to manufacture a computer to predict the likely outcome of the ball on roulette. This took a lot of people within the gaming world by surprise and led to some very worried people in high places.

Before we start talking about these "Eudaemons", I have to point out that Bass didn't succeed in making any money, not meaningful amounts, anyway. But success can be measured in many ways; for me the success of the Eudaemons isn't what was won, because there weren't any winnings to speak of. It was the fact that these methods were now deemed possible and were not science fiction but almost science fact.

Thomas Bass and his colleagues were not the first to arrive at the idea of using a computer to assist them in beating roulette. Edward Thorp used a very primitive system back in the 1960s, but without success. What Bass did was to invent a unique way of disguising a computer by hiding it in a shoe. Bass and his team took the next step from Thorp by using a micro-processor. Bass could detect certain impulses in his feet that would indicate what numbers to bet on.

One of his main accomplices was a man called James Farmer who was an astrophysicist at the time. But once again, like Edward Thorp over twenty years earlier, Bass, Farmer and their colleagues suffered from inadequacies in the technology of their day. Their big mistake was that they went about implementing their scam in an unnecessarily complicated way.

When the computer was working properly, it was calculated that it could attain a 44 per cent edge over the casino on every spin – nothing short of phenomenal. Even if they had succeeded, they would still have been up against the inferior roulette wheels that were in general circulation in Las Vegas at that time. But you don't need to be that sophisticated in order to beat roulette. This was a classic case of a group of highly qualified and intelligent people simply going down a blind alley and over-complicating the process. They failed because they were intelligent enough to make it work, and that was their downfall.

The Germans Are Coming

There is a report dating back to 1991 describing how two mysterious Germans went into a casino with nothing more than a wrist watch and won very significant sums of money. That casino was the Valkenburg casino in Holland, where they initially won over $50,000.

Back in their native Germany, the pair encountered serious losses, but they established a pattern of initially starting to win large sums of money and then losing most or in some cases all of it back. The arm of the European gaming police is a very long one and they observed the pattern.

It seems clear to me that the pair seriously outstayed their welcome in the casino world. They committed three glaring errors that led to their losses. First, they were too unsubtle in thei operation; second, they won too much money in the same casino; and third, they stayed too long and were victims of the casino counter measures. They quickly became very well known in Germany, Holland and Austria.

Later casino reports indicated that these two Germans had been using some kind of wrist calculator into which they inputted information. This approach intrigued me and I set out on a quest to find out the truth about what these two men from Freiburg had been up to.

I had always thought that beating roulette or attempting to beat roulette using the methods of Edward Thorp, Thomas Bass and James Farmer was beyond me. Their expertise lies in astrophysics and mathematics, two subjects of which I had no serious knowledge. Did this mean that beating roulette by ball drop-off prediction was impossible for people like me?

At first I ran up against many obstacles caused by my ignorance and naivety. In 1998, around about the time that I formed my first blackjack team, I made a significant breakthrough with my studies that led to me looking at the problem in an entirely different way. I knew that even the Huxley wheels were vulnerable, but discovering how to beat them was another matter.

I discovered that armed with certain mathematical data and nothing more than a cheap watch that had a stop watch function, a significant edge could be achieved on roulette. How much of an edge you may ask and I have to skip the question because the answer would be wrong anyway. Like I said, mathematics is not my field, but then it does not have to be in order to beat roulette.

The two German guys suffered from what many blackjack card counters suffer from: they knew the technical stuff but under-estimated the people that they were going up against. Knowing how to beat the casinos at whatever game is only half the battle. The real test is getting away with it for substantial amounts of money.

When I was active with my first blackjack team, it got to a stage where so many people knew what the set up was that we were very lucky to last as long as we did. This was why I figured that the best way to earn money out of this was to train people so that they could do it themselves. At least that way you are not dependent on your entire income being in the balance and hoping that certain people can keep their mouths shut.

The German duo suffered counter measure after counter measure of dealers spinning the ball super fast and dealers not accepting any bets after the ball had spun – a tactic that any casino does not really want to introduce as it slows down the number of spins per hour. But had they been more clandestine then it is possible that these two would have won a very considerable sum of money. But they proved one very important thing and every casino should take note: you don't need to be a scientist or qualified in advanced mathematics in order to beat roulette.

The Montgomery Brothers

Philip and Peter Montgomery went into my hall of fame towards the back end of 2004 when they surpassed the £250,000 mark by beating roulette. So what, you may say, that's nothing compared with the amounts of money that other roulette players have won down the years. Well that's true and I cannot argue, but this is 2006 and not 1906. The gaming industry is far more clued up now and getting something over on them is a substantial task these days. There is a world of difference between taking advantage of a dealer's mistake and clobbering the casino for a few quid, and doing it as a living.

As you will have guessed, "Montgomery" is not their real name, nor are they brothers, but they are still active. What method did they use to extract this money? Well, they didn't discover biased wheels and they certainly were not skilled enough to read the wheel. But they took around £25,000 per year each between 1999 and 2004 using a combination of past posting and stealing chips from other punters on roulette. There probably isn't a croupier alive who isn't aware of past posting or its cousin top hatting. But even the more experienced inspectors, pit bosses and managers are easy meat for the very best roulette mechanics.

The worst top hatters and past posters are very bad and I've caught many down the years. But I'm not naïve enough to think that many far more skilled individuals have managed to get through my defences. Dealers and inspectors don't tend to look out for people stealing chips from other punters. So long as they are not stealing from the casino then the other punters are fair game and should be looking after their own chips.

So the punters are basically defenceless and the CCTV isn't going to save them, either, simply because they will not even be aware that they have been robbed. Target selection is the first criterion for a roulette mechanic and he knows full well that when he takes the money it will not be missed. But they do it in small increments, which is really the way to go: a £5 chip here or a couple of singles there, and if they are lucky a pony (£25 chip).

These may not seem big amounts of money, but you only need to get £100 per night on five nights a week for a year to gross a tax-free £25,000. It is because the amounts are small that people get away with it. These guys are artists when it comes to past posting because they are masters of psychology and time misdirection. Casino personnel are on the lookout for past posters using high denomination chips and obvious decoy tactics, and this makes them fair game because it is exactly the opposite of what the best mechanics do.

Dealers and inspectors are easy meat when the action is very small. They visually tighten up when there is serious activity on the table. Then their attention is at its greatest. Towards the end of a night shift concentration levels start to drop not just for the staff but for many punters as well. It amazes me just how flippant people are with chips; it is as though the moment that cash is converted into chips that they seem to lose their value. The gaming industry has a lot to thank the inventor of the casino chip for.

The design of roulette, the shape of the table, the position of the dealer and the position of the wheel is great for cheating moves and this was how the Montgomery brothers made their living. Even the dealing procedures themselves present many avenues for attack. Despite the fact that the management continually tries to watch and motivate staff to do their job to the best of their ability, it is a fruitless task. The job is too repetitive and this is something that's very difficult to combat. The worst staff are those who are most experienced; they have seen and done it all before and if anything happens on the table then they just pay it most of the time anyway.

The mentality of the gaming staff is a very important weapon for a roulette mechanic because they thrive on carelessness and lethargy. You can easily get away with putting £1 on the number after the ball has dropped. This is £35 for about a few seconds' work and you are well on your way to your £100 a night figure. Even if you get suspected then the casino thinks "So what, it is only thirty-five quid". This is exactly what a mechanic wants you to think.

Croupier complacency can never be properly combated unless you do away with the human element altogether. Many casinos are going down the route of using electronic roulette wheels but the human dealers will always remain. Many punters prefer the interaction and electronic roulette turns an awful lot of people off the game.

In all this time, the Montgomery brothers have never been caught. Their speciality is past posting with 25p colour chips that conceal a £1 chip underneath for the other team member to claim. Obviously they are not seen to be together in the eyes of the staff, but they operate as a highly effective unit. The gaming world has certainly not seen the last of Philip and Peter Montgomery.

The Salmon

During the time that I worked inside my first casino in my home town between 1989 and 1994, there was a guy who nearly always took money from us on roulette. At that time I was heavily into blackjack and the first book that I ever read on that subject was the pivotal *Beat the Dealer*, by Edward Thorp. In that book, there was an account of one of the earliest known card counters. No one knew his name but the local dealers nicknamed him The Salmon.

The reason for this nickname was because salmon swim against the flow of the river by swimming upstream. This blackjack player was doing precisely that by consistently winning when all about him were losing. This nickname struck a chord with me because this was exactly what a guy was doing to us on roulette.

I didn't even know his name and I'm certain that the casino was unaware of just how much he was ahead in the five years that I was there. What made it worse was that the guy was so utterly annoying and the last person in the world that you wanted to see win. He was fat and balding and although he was never abusive, he just had a really annoying way about him, which is hard to explain. The reason why the casino never clocked him was because he never bought in for enough to get on the spender sheets and he never cashed out enough to get noticed.

But he turned £10 into £100 so often that he became almost legendary in my eyes. How did I know that he was constantly winning? Simple, because I was clocking him even though the casino wasn't. Why was I doing this? For personnel interest, and I had another member of staff helping me, who would clock him on my days off.

In the space of a year the guy was ahead by about £20,000, which was a truly astronomical figure for the amount of action that he generated. While he did lose, it was rare, and his losses were always miniscule. Once or twice he would appear on the cashout sheet when his winnings exceeded his usual wins. I remember one occasion quite clearly; he had been watching me spin for about thirty minutes before eventually tossing a 50p chip onto number 17.

The moment he did it I knew that the ball would be close to 17 and this was on a John Huxley mark IV wheel, as I recall, which is a very high performance wheel. As the ball fell from the track into the area where number 17 was, I was mesmerised by the ball and was hardly paying attention to the layout as I should have been. There it was coming to rest in number 17 and it pained me to put the dolly on the number and pay him.

In the space of fifteen minutes, he had parlayed that 50p into £600 before he cashed in. As soon as I knew that this guy was not winning by luck, I set about trying to find out what was doing. He motivated me to find out the truth about roulette and how to read the spin. I had practised trying to hit certain blocks and spin out of certain blocks before, but without much success. This time would be different, because I was now conducting my own exhaustive study of roulette. Within six months I had figured out how to beat the game, but the problem was that I couldn't manage to do it consistently. I knew that I was dramatically altering the odds in my favour whenever I was dealing, which meant that I could also reverse that effect.

But The Salmon seemed to be doing something that I wasn't, because he was far more successful at it than I was and he never played the same numbers, so there was no chance whatsoever that he had discovered a bias. Suddenly a thought struck me like a bolt of lightening, oh my god why did it take so long to realise this...? What a dummy! Now I knew why The Salmon was being far more successful than me: he was sticking to the same wheel.

I thought back to all the times that I had seen him and he only ever seemed to play on American Roulette 1. Suddenly the thought that each particular wheel was behaving and performing independently from the others became apparent to me. Yes, that was it, this was why my results were erratic. I was trying to do too much, I was trying to remember the characteristics of six American roulette wheels at once while The Salmon was only remembering one.

One night after we had closed, the duty manager ordered a shuffling of the wheels and the wheel that had been positioned on AR1 was relocated to another table. The following night, The Salmon came in and went straight to AR1 as usual and I watched him intently from the other side of the pit to see if he would notice the difference in the wheel. The fact that he looked puzzled and was looking around the pit told me that he knew that something wasn't right.

He systematically inspected all the other wheels until he

found the wheel that had been on AR1. As it happened, that table was yet to be opened but The Salmon hung about well past his bedtime until it was. Within ten minutes of it opening he was £200 ahead, having only bought in for £20. When I eventually left this casino in 1994, The Salmon was still winning money and will likely continue to do so. I never encountered him again because he never came in any other casino where I worked, but I didn't need to see again because now I knew his secret! But fate would bring us together anyway, as we met by chance when I was out shopping one afternoon.

Mr Leigh and His Merry Men (and Women)

What you are about to read did actually happen, and in my opinion did so purely thanks to short-term luck and nothing else. So why then should I put Norman Leigh and his system players onto my list of heroes of roulette if all they did was get lucky using a randon system? They are here for reasons other than making money.

First, Norman Leigh became public enemy number one in the eyes of the French casinos in 1966 because he won the substantial figure of FF800,000, which at the time was worth £58,000 – a very tidy sum forty years ago. Second, he scared the French gaming industry so much that they barred him from every casino in France. Third, he had the guts and determination to hit back at an industry that had wronged him by treating his father badly.

The facts that Norman Leigh and his "reverse Labouchere" betting system has no proven long-term mathematical edge, and that he was only active for about two weeks and would have surely lost it back had his team continued, are neither here nor there. But what cannot be ignored is that his name went into roulette folklore because of what he did and his account of it in the wonderful book *Thirteen Against the Bank*. This tells the story of Leigh and his team of twelve individuals from all walks of life who took on the might of the Casino Municipal in Nice and broke the bank.

The term "breaking the bank" does not mean busting the casino. It means taking all the chips that are currently on the roulette table – a fair sum of money but nothing compared with the financial resources of a large casino.

The only reason that the French casinos gave for barring Leigh's team was because they won systematically, consistently and methodically. Norman Leigh was born in 1928 in London and did his national service in 1946. He worked as an interpreter for a while but retained a lifelong fascination with roulette. Because Leigh was sent to prison for fraud in 1968, I've read comments from people who think that Leigh was a con man who tricked twelve individuals into bankrolling a trip to Monte Carlo in 1966 while he basically free rolled with their money.

I don't buy this, simply because the era that we are talking about is 1966 and not 2006. I think it is more likely that Leigh firmly believed in his own mind that his system was viable, which made the task of selling it to others a lot easier. I know from personal experience that casinos will bar players if they are winning too much money and especially if they don't fully understand the reasons behind why they are winning.

Because Leigh was winning in 1966 and not 2006, I believe that the casinos acted through fear brought about through ignorance. Modern-day casinos tolerate system players and even encourage them by placing score cards and writing equipment at the side of the table to assist them. They understand that there is no mathematical system available that can beat them and that they will eventually get the system players' money.

The casinos knew only too well about betting systems back in the 1960s, but were not overly aware of the strange looking "reverse Labouchere" system, which is vastly different from the normal progression type systems. A two-week period is a very short amount of time to prove the validity of whether a betting system is working or not, so the fact that Leigh and his team won nearly £60,000 is academic.

The game was terminated by the casino when Leigh's team was £58,000 ahead, which is a vastly different story. The gaming world is full of punters who have been ahead by astronomical amounts, only to lose it back. I could fill an entire book with stories of punters and even system players who were ahead for considerable lengths of time only to be wiped out by one big reverse; every casino employee in the world has similar stories.

But although casinos tolerate system players, they are not overly fond of them because they tend to bleed small amounts of money for long periods without giving anything back in return by way of action on other games. System players tend to be very careful with their expenditure and don't get involved in any other game apart from roulette. In short, they are not interested in any other casino activity other than the one game where they can execute their system.

The best systems can defer loss for very long periods indeed, and it is this strange quirk that creates the illusion that some of them work. The Labouchere system is one such system, named after of one Queen Victoria's ministers. The "reverse Labouchere" turns the normal system requirement of adding to the bet after a loss on its head. It essentially only increases the bet when you are already ahead, but it does require significant starting capital to operate effectively.

Leigh came across this system while scouring a bookshop near Charing Cross so it wasn't his idea; he merely copied it with a few added modifications of his own thrown in. In today's more enlightened times, it is doubtful whether a man like Leigh could have convinced twelve seemingly intelligent individuals to go on a caper like this (but then again). But back in the 1960s, the overwhelming majority of people had next to no experience of this kind of thing and had certainly not read about anything to do with the game of roulette.

But the determination of Leigh was something that I've always admired, especially after reading his book. If you can accept the fact that some of the events have been enhanced for literary effect, the book is a very enjoyable read. After getting hold of his system in a local bookshop, Leigh's next step was to recruit a team.

This was the clever part about what Leigh did in my opinion; he knew full well that the system would require a fair degree of starting capital and that a bigger team would accelerate any winning run should they have one. A single person using the "reverse Labouchere" system could have taken weeks if not months to get wiped out, but could also have taken a long time to encounter one of the progression "mushrooms" as they called them in the book.

Leigh systematically interviewed every team member after placing an advertisement in a Bournemouth newspaper and then placing further advertisements in national newspapers for what he called "a limited number of vacancies of a clerical nature in a group to be formed on the Cote d'Azur". The entire operation from the planning to the wording of the advertisement in the newspapers to the training and then execution of the system was almost military-like in its execution.

This team play really spooked the casinos in France; they had never encountered anything like it before. But forming a team and attacking the casinos systematically is something that I can relate to and anyone who has read my book *Princes of Darkness: The World of Highstakes Blackjack* will know what I am talking about. Each team member walked away with almost $12,000 (£4,230) profit, which was a substantial sum in 1966, but their greatest achievement was to scare the French gaming industry so much that the French government got involved at one stage.

As soon as Leigh's book was published, he received offers to take his system to Las Vegas from numerous people, but he declined – draw your own conclusions. But I take my hat off to a very intelligent and determined man who had the guts to take on an industry and stand tall under what must have been intense pressure and very close scrutiny and come out standing tall: Norman Leigh... I salute you.

CHAPTER 2

HOW ROULETTE WHEELS BECOME BIASED

In the previous chapter we talked about certain players who made very substantial amounts of money by discovering and then exploiting biased wheels. In this chapter we will consider how a wheel becomes biased. What we are entering into is a very complex subject, as many of the reasons for bias are a mystery even today to modern roulette wheel engineers.

But despite the advances in roulette wheel technology and construction, the problem with biased wheels is real and still exploitable. The casino hierarchy does not want this kind of information getting out and with very good reason. But we had at least one biased wheel to my knowledge at the first casino that I worked in and another at the second. Like a fool, I never exploited this situation until after I had left gaming, which is something that still niggles me, but I've wised up a lot since those early days.

I've read confidential reports on roulette wheels that indicate to me that for a roulette wheel to be totally random it needs to be flawless and perfect in every single way. This is an impossibility because a roulette wheel is just too complicated for it to reach anywhere near perfection.

There are a lot more components to a roulette wheel than

meet the eye. Nearly all of the modern roulette wheels that are manufactured today are highly tuned pieces of equipment; whether they are the latest models by John Huxley or the Paulsen or Paul Tramble wheels, the quality is exceptionally high in them all. But bias still appears and will continue to appear.

The major problem is that whenever the technicians service these wheels, they tend to look only for identifiable faults. This means faults that they can understand and are trained to detect. Many times down the years casino officials have detected biased wheels but still couldn't find what the fault was. In my mind, we have the makings of a problem here that can only partly be solved by science.

There are forces at work that are taking effect on roulette wheels, which as yet we don't fully understand. Because we don't understand them, we can't detect them, but that does not mean that they are not present. I was doing some research a few years ago on "temporary bias" on roulette wheels. My studies were merely supposition but I believe that it is possible that a roulette wheel could be influenced over time by outside forces or even temperature differences.

Physical abnormalities are easily spotted by the casino, or at least they should be. I've worked in casinos where the frets (number dividers) and canoes (diamond-shaped ball deflectors in the balltrack) have been loose and I've even pulled them out on occasion. Of course this should never have been allowed to happen but it does highlight just how certain casinos fail miserably when it comes to wheel maintenance.

But the most that any roulette wheel manufacturer can achieve is to produce a wheel that is "almost random". The word "almost" leaves an area that is as potentially exploitable to roulette as card counting and shuffle tracking are to blackjack.

Most of the time that 2.7 per cent house edge (single zero roulette) is more than enough to take care of any small bias that may exist anyway, and even though a number may be appearing more than it should, it may still not be occurring often enough to give the player an advantage.

But the main point here is that if a small bias does exist then it only takes a series of accidental events to swing this into a full blown player advantage, providing that it is identified. But identifying it or even trying to identify it is beyond the scope or the patience of the overwhelming majority of punters. The vast majority of them who even bother to look at all arrive at incorrect conclusions anyway, as detecting true bias as opposed to imagined bias is not straightforward.

The main factor that causes wheel bias is repetitive wear and tear, either by the wheel being in motion for long hours or through the operation of it by the dealer. It is only manufactured from wood and metal and they are hardly impervious materials. This constant use is a factor in why the wheels are relocated within the casino periodically although it is far from being the only reason, as I've already stated.

A wheel that's on a left-handed table will incur usage differently than a wheel on a right-handed table, and vice versa. Recently, there have been developments in the field of bias detection with firms manufacturing bias detection software. In fact the new Saturn wheels that are in circulation now can be fitted with inbuilt memory; it is incorporated into the base of the wheel and can record data for up to six years. The Saturn data logger theoretically detects bias whether it is caused by inaccurate wheel balancing, table movement or whatever. Permanent bias is simple to detect and it does not take that long to find. Temporary bias is more difficult to detect and therefore casinos are vulnerable. This introduces the very shady area of wheel tampering.

The people who have direct access to the wheels are casino employees, in whatever capacity. Because the level of action inside an average UK casino is not that big, casino management staff tend to let their guard down with regard to these things. Replacing very expensive roulette wheels or having them rebuilt is hardly an acceptable option for many casinos, especially if that wheel is a consistent money earner. If strict security procedures were always adhered to then casinos wouldn't be cheated as often as they are. They may have the game sewn up by having an unbeatable edge in their favour, but that assumes that the roulette player is playing by their rules.

If everyone in the world played roulette the way that the gaming industry wanted you to play it there would be no medium- to long-term winners and your positive expectation would always be negative. Luckily you don't have to play by their rules, but if you don't then casinos will bar you from playing or possibly even prosecute you if they catch you cheating.

But the overwhelming number of biased wheels happen purely and simply by accident rather than through some underhandedness by employees or punters. A wheel can be biased in numerous ways. The ball drop-off point from the ball track can be repeatedly in the same place, although this is a characteristic that very rarely crops up these days on modern wheels. Rarely, not never – please don't expect the dealers or inspectors to notice this either. They couldn't care less and wouldn't know a biased wheel if one dropped on their head. With the use of bias detection programmes then anyone can identify a biased wheel, but the real skill is to be able to identify one without the use of software and to be 100 per cent sure that what you've located is *true* bias.

The reason why this particular bias is so crucial isn't because if it exists you can necessarily identify numbers that will come up, as the Billy Walters' team did, for instance. But having a consistent ball drop-off point significantly aids a player's ability to be able to read the spin. In fact, based on just how lax the casino was where I first worked, it seems highly likely now to me that this particular flaw may have been the major reason for the success of The Salmon.

Any part of a roulette wheel that comprises metal can be subject to bias effect. This means that a very large percentage of the wheel is vulnerable to any kind of outside force that effects metal. In that wheel we have numerous components, like the wheel head, spindle, turret, frets, canoes and so on, and each component can be a potential bias waiting to happen.

Another major factor in bias forming on roulette is whether or not the wheel is level. Any bias may or may not be accentuated by the wheel not being totally level. This is another avenue where temporary bias can and does occur. The following chapter tells the true account of modern biased wheel play in England and Europe over the past few years, it is the true story of Rashid Khan.

Chapter 3

The Rashid Khan Success Story

Rashid Khan first telephoned me in the summer of 2003 just after I had moved house again with my girlfriend Angela. By this time I had been out of blackjack for about a year and had been playing poker professionally online in that time. I was enjoying online poker, and still do, but it just doesn't give me a buzz like beating the casinos does.

I had been semi-involved with blackjack and roulette teams over the past eighteen months or so, as I had trained several teams and individuals in that time. But what made this story so unique for me was that the success was achieved against what are in my opinion the finest roulette wheels on the market today... the John Huxley wheels, of which the Saturn is an absolute gem.

As it happened Rashid Khan knew a friend of someone whom I had trained. It was amazing now how many people were aware not only that I existed but also of who I was. It would have been exceptionally naïve of me to think that gaming industry personnel were at the very least not aware of me or my name.

But I knew full well that something was amiss when I tried to gain access to a couple of casinos in my home town without success. This was at a time when I was in frequent contact with several ex-croupiers who were freely gaining access to these clubs and punting without hindrance. The casinos knew that they were ex-gaming and allowed them to play freely… not so yours truly. So the cat was out of the bag somewhat, but that was certainly not going to curtail my plans. The casinos might have been able to stop my entry or prevent me from playing but they couldn't take away what I knew.

Rashid Khan was a successful businessman from Sutton Coldfield but spent most of his time in the north of England. He and three of his business colleagues were seriously interested in attacking biased roulette wheels for big amounts of money. Rashid knew an acquaintance of mine called Mark Goodwin, whom I had trained in beating blackjack games with shuffling machines.

The phone rang at 7.30pm but it came as no surprise because I was expecting Rashid's call. "Hello is that Carl?"

"Speaking."

"My name's Rashid Khan. Mark said that it was OK to call you at home."

"Hi Rashid. Mark told me a bit about you."

We made small talk for about five minutes, which is something that I loathe. If something is on the agenda and has to be said then I'm always happier when it is being said. I knew perfectly well what Rashid wanted, anyway, because Mark had filled me in. Rashid knew an awful lot about the inner workings of casinos but wasn't prepared to divulge to me at this stage how he knew what he knew. But what he did know or at least suspected was that the roulette wheels were not as random as the casinos were making them out to be, and that included the John Huxley wheels.

Rashid was also aware of what counter measures he would have to employ in order to escape detection. He was intending to use numerous bettors to get the action across. He knew full well that I had the information that he wanted. He already knew about biased wheels and an awful lot about what exactly made them bias, which intrigued me greatly, as this is knowledge that's not widely known. But what he lacked was the information to identify whether or not a wheel was in fact biased and not just showing some normal random distribution of numbers. The human brain is very good at being able to spot patterns and this is a serious problem because, most of the time, we see "patterns" that are emerging which are entirely normal.

People do it all the time with everyday things – lottery numbers, birthdays and so on. People see everyday occurrences or witness what they believe to be something remarkable and they immediately interpret it as something other than what it really is: a normal mathematical occurrence. But despite the complexities of the human brain, it can in fact be easily fooled. Rashid Khan came across to me as a very clever individual and nobody's fool, and he was more than aware of these mind tricks. In no way was he in the mood to chase fool's gold.

"Mark informs me that you might have information that I need," said Rashid, in a very business-like let's-stop-making-small-talk kind of a way.

"It all depends on just what kind of information you are looking for, Rashid."

"What I need is the data to be able to detect if a series of numbers is revealing a true bias or not, and Mark tells me that you have a computer program that does this. Is that correct?"

"Yes it is."

"Will you help me with some data that I have?" asked

Rashid. As it turned out, he had access to 10,000 roulette numbers taken from four roulette wheels inside a casino in the midlands.

"Before we go any further, Rashid, do you know that these wheels are biased?" I replied.

"No," he said curtly.

"Well, 10,000 numbers sounds a lot and it is a lot but it is still only taken from four wheels. The chances are very slim that one of these four wheels is biased enough to provide you with a meaningful edge."

"Why do you say that? Mark told me that you once told him that biased wheels are forming all the time for many different reasons, and that the casinos can't combat it fully."

"That's right, but the latest wheel technology is making them harder and harder to find. I'll be honest with you, the chances that you have data that highlights a biased wheel are very slim."

"So you are saying that I'm wasting my time?"

"No not at all, what I'm saying is that you have to spread your net a bit wider than this. Where did you get these numbers from?" I enquired. Rashid chuckled and made some derisive comment to the effect that it was none of my business. I didn't press him on a subject that he was very reticent to discuss.

"If I photocopy the data and get it across to you can you run a check on the numbers?" he asked.

"Yeah, sure, but over what time frame were these numbers taken and how can you be sure that they were taken on the same wheel?" I replied. Rashid went silent for a few seconds before finally revealing that he was 100 per cent certain that they were taken from the same wheel. I explained to him how casinos moved wheels around after closing time and that he needed to be certain that the data matched the respective wheels. Despite my protestations, he was adamant that these numbers came from four different wheels and that these wheels could be identified.

"So how have you come by these numbers, Rashid, at thirty spins per hour? You don't strike me as the type of person to sit around for several hundred hours taking numbers down." Despite getting rebuffed earlier on this point, it intrigued me how he had come by these numbers. Asian punters simply don't sit around for hour after hour taking numbers down on roulette; it's simply not their style.

In my mind there were three possibilities. First, he might have got someone else to do his dirty work, which seemed likely. Second, he might have scavenged these numbers from system players who had been logging them, but this explanation didn't seem likely to me as he couldn't be sure that they had not been duped by a wheel switch. So he couldn't trust the data of a punter that he didn't even know.

But there was a third and more sinister possibility: this guy just seemed to have too much inside gaming knowledge for my liking and the prospect of him being a casino mole crossed my mind more than once. Maybe I was just being paranoid; in fact as I was listening to him there was a fourth possibility that occurred to me – that he may have had someone on the inside providing him with the data.

One thing was for sure, he wasn't going to divulge too much to me at this stage. "Let's just say that I have my sources."

"And you are certain that these numbers are from the same wheels?"

"Certain."

"Is it possible to send them by e-mail, Rashid?"

"It is, Carl, but I would rather bring them in person. Besides, I would like to talk to you some more about this as I'm planning a trip into Europe shortly."

"Oh, anywhere nice?"

"I have some friends in Holland in a place called Sluis. I think that there may be a little roulette action over there, so I need some information from you before I go."

We made some more small talk for about ten minutes before terminating the conversation. Rashid had asked if he could come round to my house in person and I had agreed, somewhat reluctantly. I normally like to keep my business separate from my home life and away from my partner. The only thing that she sees of what I do is my writing and online poker. I sat thinking about my meeting with Rashid; this was the first time that anyone outside my usual contacts was visiting me at home and I was starting to think about the potential ramifications of that.

Well, too late to worry about that now, I should have thought about it sooner. What we had not discussed over the phone, though we should have, was the subject of money. At the end of the day, he wanted information from me and that information sure don't come free in my business. Nobody had approached me this way before and I sat there thinking about how much I was going to charge Rashid. If I went too high then I would lose him as he would likely try and get the information from somewhere else, but for a lot less. I sat there and contemplated many things, the worst of which was that Rashid Khan wasn't his real name and he was an undercover casino agent… and I had invited him to my house!

The Distinguished Businessman

I had managed to talk Angela into seeing some of her friends on the night that Rashid Khan was due to visit. I knew full well what he wanted from me and I also knew full well what I was going to give him, but for how much? I had finally decided on a figure which was adequate for the information that he wanted. Plus I was certain that he would struggle to get the information of detecting bias from anywhere else, especially in the time frame that he wanted it.

I must admit to feeling quite nervous, but who was to blame for that? I really must try to curb this impulsive tendency that I have towards flirting with danger. It will get me into serious trouble one day, of that I'm sure. Then I started to think about how much more money I could make if I took a percentage of Rashid's winnings; only problem was… how could I trust a man whom I had never met in my life?

I knew for a fact that he would barter with me and I was a long way from being the world's greatest negotiator. Haggling just wasn't my style – once I've fixed a price on something then they either pay my price or they hit the highway, it is as simple as that.

At 7:30pm there was a faint knock at the front door, so faint that I could barely hear it over the television. I answered the door and facing me was a diminutive Pakistani fellow around five foot five with a thick moustache and shoulder length curly hair.

"Hi Carl, Rashid Khan, pleased to meet you," he said, reaching out to shake hands with me.

"Hi Rashid, come on in. Did you find the address easily enough?"

"Yeah, your directions were spot on."

We once again made small talk over a coffee and I discovered that Rashid Khan was thirty-eight years of age and had five chil-

children. He came across as a very articulate and educated man, a pleasure to talk to and not the least bit threatening.

"Have you ever thought about going back into blackjack?"

"Once or twice but playing poker online is easy and I don't have to watch my back. I'm earning more money without having to go out of the house," I responded.

"You would like to go back though, wouldn't you, Carl? Staring at a computer screen is not you, is it?" said Rashid.

This guy had me pegged immediately. He knew that I was far from happy doing what I was doing now. Poker was all right but once you've cracked the hard part of winning money consistently then it gets to become a grind and online limit hold'em is just that... a grind! I wanted to recreate the buzz of beating the casinos again, and if I couldn't find the time or get the access to any of them then at least I was going to hit them in another way, by sharing what I knew with people who did have the time and who could get access. Besides, things are different now. I have Angela in my life and it would be grossly unfair on her if I was away at night or playing in some other part of the country and staying away from home for days at a time.

"How does this computer program work?" asked Rashid.

"It looks at numbers and assesses whether they are occurring more or less than what is normal mathematical variance. It then compiles frequency distribution charts, which tells me what numbers are coming, and also what numbers are coming that are neighbours of the other frequent numbers and whether or not those frequencies are normal. You see, Rashid, it is simply not enough to detect a single number that's appearing more than the rest."

"Why is that?"

"Because a single number could easily be an anomaly and these new Huxley wheels are so good that you can't narrow down single numbers anyway. If you identify bias on a Huxley wheel it is likely to be a section bias rather than an outright number bias."

"So how did you come by this program?"

"I have my sources as well, Rashid."

"I need to know if this program will do precisely what you are saying that it will do. Could I have a demonstration of it?"

"Sure, but I would still like to know how you came by these numbers… do you have someone on the inside?" I remarked. I wasn't letting go of this curious point and fired the question at Rashid looking him squarely in the eye. I got just the reaction that I was expecting from him.

Before he had chance to answer my question I hit him with another one. "Are you getting this data from electronic read-outs?"

Rashid's silence coupled with his smile told me all that I needed to know. He had someone on the inside who was passing him the data. This meant that data could be relied on to be accurate.

"Like I said, Carl, I have my sources," remarked Rashid, with a boyish, cheeky smile, which confirmed to me that I had well and truly hit the nail on the head.

"Well, it is none of my business," I responded, but I was happy now that I knew the truth. Not because it would do me any good – it was just because I was such a nosey parker and it would have killed me not to know. So curiosity never got to kill the cat in this instance and I could sleep easily tonight. This would explain why Rashid was so enamoured with this bunch of numbers, they were not just any old numbers. These numbers were passed to him by someone who already suspected that the wheel was biased and was passing this information on to someone who had the money and the contacts to do something about it.

This put an entirely different slant on things. It meant that Rashid had access to inside knowledge and could very easily cut me out of the equation if I over-priced the information that I was giving him. After all, this stuff may not be common knowledge but it sure as hell is not unique to me. Anyone with an advanced qualification in mathematics or statistics would be able to arrive at the same answer without the use of any computer program.

Rashid and I made small talk once again for about twenty minutes before I finally showed him the computer program. He watched as I explained the process, what it did and how it arrived at its calculations. I also gave him a dummy practice run with a set of deliberately produced numbers, which indicated a bias on a factitious wheel. What I didn't tell him was just how short a time it is before a wheel begins to show signs of bias. I wasn't going to tell him anything that would mean him cutting me out of the equation in future.

"How do I get hold of a program like this, Carl?"

"Very difficult, I don't know if you can as there are not that many in existence of this type."

"So how did you come by it then?"

"Like I said, I have my contacts," I replied evasively, once again.

When I had given Rashid the demonstration and he had presented me with the numbers, we spoke about how much it would cost him to buy this information. Rashid was a silver-tongued skilled negotiator and I must confess that he ended up paying a damn sight less that what I had planned. Still, it was basically money for nothing and I had barely had to do anything in order to get it.

"Do you think that it is possible for there to be some sort of temporary bias on a roulette wheel?" Rashid asked.

"What do you mean by temporary?" I knew the answer to his question but I just wanted to be certain about what he meant.

"I mean exactly that, a temporary bias that is only present for a very short length of time. So short that the casino can't pick up on it."

"Do you mean accidental bias or deliberate?"

"Both."

"Of course it's possible, I was doing some research on atmospheric and heat effects on roulette wheels a while back, but couldn't prove anything. But deliberate manmade bias is easily achievable. In fact this would be impossible to detect if the reason for the bias had disappeared afterwards. This would also get around any casino that had bias detection software of its own because there is no way that a piece of software could detect a bias that was only happening over the space of a few hours. Why do you ask, Rashid?"

"Oh it's just something that I have in the pipeline; I'll get back to you at a later date on that one, Carl."

Rashid left a short while later after I promised to have the results of his 10,000 numbers for him the following day. He had set me thinking, though. Difficult as this was, it was still a damn sight more exciting than playing online poker. Stuff like this always gives me a buzz, whereas internet poker bores the pants off me at times. But Rashid Khan had something about him – a steely determination that I once had had, and I could see an awful lot of myself in him. Don't know if that's good or bad?

The Results

I awoke at 6:30am the following morning and immediately Rashid Khan was in my head. I hate lying in bed at the best of times but doubly so when I'm on a mission. I had promised Rashid that I would get him the results by this evening so I had work to do. By 1pm I had the answers. The first and second batch of numbers that had been taken from two separate wheels in two different casinos both proved negative.

The fourth batch started off showing signs of promise and seemed to indicate that there was possibly something that wasn't quite right. But the problem is that even if there is a bias on a wheel, it has to be strong enough to overcome the house edge, and most biased wheels are not. This is what makes the Huxley wheels so damn good, because even when one is faulty, it isn't enough to overcome the 2.7 per cent edge against you.

But the result of the third batch was something else: smack bang in the centre of the tier numbers was a batch of six numbers that were appearing at an alarming rate. Those numbers were 36, 11, 30, 8, 23 and 10. When you take one individual number in isolation, that number can randomly be expected to arrive at a rate of one number for every thirty-seven spins. This means that the number will come up on average 2.7 times per hundred or 2.7 per cent of the time.

Over the space of 3,000 spins, these six numbers had come up no fewer than 972 times. This works out at an average of 5.4 per cent per number, which is double what the normal distribution should have been. The lowest percentage of the six was number 23, which was arriving at a rate of 4.88 per cent, but number 30 was coming in at a whopping 6.27 per cent. I ran these figures through the data check screen, which indicated that the chance of these numbers appearing by accident over this many spins was less than 1 per cent.

I telephoned Rashid that evening with the news and he seemed very excited by it. So excited in fact that he almost divulged the name of the casino to me. He had already said too much and I was now certain that this casino wasn't far south of where I lived. However, this was his business and his venture. I wished him the very best of luck and gave him a few tips on spreading his action and the counter measures the casino could employ against him.

He thanked me for my efforts and help and we parted with me thinking that this could possibly be the last that I would ever hear or see of one Mr Rashid Khan... how wrong I was.

The Return

About three weeks later Rashid telephoned me completely out of the blue. I had been out for a meal with Angela and when I got back there was a message on my mobile phone. It was Rashid and he wanted to speak to me as soon as possible. At first I thought that it was bad news, those results that I had given him had resulted in him and his associates losing a lot of money... shit and now he knew where I lived. I was thinking all kinds of horrible things, mainly about what Rashid and his accomplices were going to do to me. It was late but rather than wait until the morning to call him, curiosity was getting the better of me and I called him straight back.

"Hi, is that Rashid? It's Carl... I've just got your message."

Rashid's voice was very cheerful and upbeat and this relaxed me as I realised that he wasn't calling me with bad news. As it turned out, I had been totally off the mark in my speculation about where Rashid had been going to play. He had in fact been to Holland. I knew that he had friends there, because he had told me so earlier, but I didn't know that he was intending to play roulette there and especially this soon.

Rashid informed me that he had won $20,000 playing rou-
lette in an unlicensed casino in Holland over the space of a couple of nights. He had encountered a few problems with the
owner and it looked at one stage as if he would be seriously
harmed when he was physically threatened by the owner and
his heavies. Presumably for winning the money and also for being an outsider and winning the money. I asked him what make
of wheel it was and he told me that he couldn't remember but
he knew that it wasn't a Huxley. This meant that Rashid had
done well but nowhere near as well as if the wheel had been a
Huxley wheel.

"Listen, Carl, I may need some more information from you in
the future, I'm planning a trip into Germany soon or possibly
France and I need your services. You've convinced me that your
data is accurate. We would have beat the bastards for a lot more
had they not put the stop on us."

"Listen to me, Rashid, you were lucky to get out of there by
all accounts. Dodgy back-street joints are really not where you
should be playing."

Rashid laughed and said, "Yeah, but they can't afford Huxley
wheels can they?"

The man had a point. It sounded to me that this place was
ripe for picking off. The only thing that Rashid had not bar-
gained for was getting beaten up, or worse. Still, the lesson was
learned and if he ever encountered the same situation again he
would take his own heavies, and he knew plenty. At least my
information had been very profitable to him, which was good
for his sake and also for mine.

"Do you know, when you said the other week that a bias on
roulette could be manufactured for a very short length of time
so that any casino couldn't pick it up…?"

"Yes."

"Well I would like to know a bit more about how to go about that. Is it something that you could tell me about, out of the goodness of your heart?" replied Rashid, cheekily insinuating that I should tell him for nothing. It was obvious that Rashid and I needed to meet again, and soon. Rashid had this fixation with getting an angle, especially in gambling arenas. But what he was doing was not gambling but earning money in the same way that I was earning money playing online poker.

Once you reach a situation where you achieve a 100 per cent plus payback, you are no longer gambling but earning money. The only difference is that employed people in normal jobs know exactly how much money they will receive at the end of the month, whereas professional punters have no idea, rather like other self-employed individuals.

Once you can get your head around the fluctuations, you've cracked it. Rashid was no more gambling than I was whenever I played poker, or the punter who has inside knowledge that a certain horse will not be racing to win today and therefore lays the thing to lose on the betting exchanges. He never risked a bean unless he knew that he could beat the game, which is exactly as it should be, unless your second name is Mug.

But to cut a long story short, we never had the chance to meet at that time as Rashid was busy doing other things, but I knew that we would be in contact again very soon, because men like him don't let things go once they have got their teeth into something.

Europe Take Two

All this was starting to feel like "groundhog day" when Rashid telephoned me some while later with another set of numbers that he wanted me to run the rule over. Once again these numbers were taken from wheels in Europe and I had the feeling that this was the trip to France and Germany that Rashid had been talking about earlier.

Damn, I wish that I had this man's contacts. How he was getting these numbers from so far away was a puzzle to me. Surely he didn't have insiders in casinos hundreds of miles away? But then again, I wouldn't put anything past him. He kind of reminded me of Steve, my financial backer for my first blackjack team. The same sort of shady business-like individual with contacts all over the place. I mean, I was in gaming for nigh on ten years and I didn't have the contacts that he had.

Rashid had a group of just over 4,000 numbers taken from three wheels. I knew that the layouts on European wheels could be different from ours and bore that in mind when I inputted the data. The roulette game as it is featured in England is a rather odd mixture. The number sequences on English wheels are French where there is a single zero with the numbers 26 and 32 either side of it, but the true American wheel has 2 and 28 either side of zero and they also have the double zero wheel over there.

What we have in England is a kind of mishmash game that's half the American version and half the French. When I asked Rashid about the layout of the numbers, he told me that it was the same as it was in England. Two batches of numbers totalling 2,800 were useless, they had started off with a proportionately high number of results in the region that included the numbers 22, 18, 29, 7 and 28. But by the end of the sequence, this had totally dissipated.

This confirmed that Rashid had someone on the inside and this someone had been confused by what had been a genuinely normal flurry of numbers over the space of a few nights. The other batch of 1,200 numbers was altogether more interesting. A group of seven numbers that included 35, 3, 26, 0, 32, 15 and 19 were arriving far more often than mere chance. In an entirely normal series of 1,200 numbers, each number should arrive just over 32 times on average, with this group of numbers arriving in total about 227 times between them.

This group of numbers came up 451 times, which is almost double what the frequency should have been. But the striking thing was that each of the seven numbers came up well above the average, which meant that this wasn't just some normal anomaly in the figures. One of these seven numbers should have arisen on average once in every 5.3 spins but they were coming in at a rate of once every 2.6 spins. Over the space of 1,200 numbers, this was enough to prove that something was not quite right with that wheel. I gave Rashid the data and once again he was over the moon.

"How can you be sure that the wheel will be there when you go over?" I enquired.

"I will know, just trust me, and if it's gone, it is gone and I will have wasted a bit of time," replied Rashid in a philosophical manner.

"Fair enough," I said, not wanting to press the matter further.

"Thanks for this, Carl. I'll get back to you shortly with an idea of mine that I've been losing some sleep over."

"That's fine, but can I just ask you if these numbers have been taken from a Huxley wheel?"

"No they haven't," replied Rashid. We agreed to talk further when he got back from Europe.

A Whole New Ball Game

About six weeks went by before I heard from Rashid again. This time he informed me that he had won almost thirty grand from casinos in France and Germany before returning to England. He felt that it was like shelling peas once he found a biased wheel, and I suppose it was really. The hard part has been done but how this guy gets wind of these wheels is something else. Inside information is worth its weight in gold, always has been and always will be.

Mind you, the information has to be good and not just any old crap, but people like Rashid Khan don't need expertise. They get their hands on all the expertise they want, and money talks. I suppose what is really important for these people isn't so much what they know but what the people who they know know… if you know what I mean! They just make it their job to know people and they have an uncanny ability to convert knowing people into making money in whatever field.

I consider myself to be one of the leading experts in Europe in casino gambling and advantage play, yet I can't compete with men like Rashid when it comes to making money. They are experts in nothing but can make money while people like you and me are still pondering how. If I didn't have the gambling and poker skill and knowledge that I have, I don't know how I would make a living other than to grind it out in some mundane job working nine to five. Men like Rashid Khan will earn money whatever the area or product – they are truly ingenious.

"How did it go over there?"

"Like clockwork, but we had one hairy moment where I thought that they were on to us. Managers were actually inspecting the wheel as we were cashing out in one place."

"That's bad news, sounds like the game is up."

"Oh I wouldn't go as far as to say that."

"If they find something wrong with that wheel, and you must assume that they have, they will automatically think that you knew something. Also if they have never seen you in that casino before they will also know that someone must have given you the information to know that the wheel was biased. Your details will probably have been passed on to the European gaming police and they will be on to you."

"What are the chances of that?"

"What, you mean about them being on to you...? About 50-50 I would say."

"Yeah, but there is nothing illegal about exploiting a biased wheel; it is their own stupid fault for not spotting it first and doing something about it in my book."

"Maybe so, but they sure don't need an excuse to prevent you from playing and they don't have to give you a reason, either. In their eyes, you are a smart, clued-up punter and that makes you their enemy, it is as simple as that. I think, Rashid, that you need either to act very quickly if you know about any more biased wheels or to use a third party to get the action across."

"I had already thought of that. In fact I've a couple of colleagues who are willing to come on board with this."

"You know that the John Huxley wheels will be a totally different ball game don't you?"

"Yeah, so you've said, but you know that I told you about this idea that I had before I went away, Carl."

"Yeah."

"Well I would like to meet you and talk about this some more, if that's fine with you. I'm a bit tied up for the rest of the week but early next week would be good for me."

Well I'm free most nights, so whatever night we agreed would be fine by me. I must confess to having been curious about what Rashid's idea was to beat the low profile Huxley wheels but, knowing him, it would be good.

Ingenuity Rears Its Head

As usual Rashid was punctual and arrived at precisely the time we had agreed. I had been staring out of the living room window as I often do when contemplating something important. Rashid's black Mercedes SL 500 pulled up outside. The fact that his car was black seemed to add to the mystique surrounding him.

Once again Angela was out with friends and in fact we had been arguing shortly before Rashid was due to arrive. She didn't like the thought of what she called "people like him" coming round to our house. She had got Rashid pegged as some type of mobster with his black car and long black overcoat. He would have made a good debt collector because he certainly looked the part.

I hated arguing with Angela but in the cold light of day I had to concede that she had a point. It was perfectly possible that I could be getting myself into serious hot water by mixing in the circles that I was mixing in now. But it all seemed terribly exciting once again and I was starting to recreate the buzz that I had from blackjack. Despite the fact that I wasn't present when Rashid was busy doing his stuff, I didn't need to be as I was there in spirit and my knowledge and expertise were there as well.

I suppose that this was what Angela found hard to understand. She had her own successful business and I think that she forgets that I need something as well – the thrill of the chase, with the goal being another casino scalp. I need more than a job. Beating the middle limit games online was proving to be a bit of a no brainer. Sure I would have my bad spells like any other poker player, but I had never had a losing month.

The bottom line is that I know that I'll be ahead at the end of any one month and that kind of takes the edge off it. But that's what poker is, it is a job like any other. Rashid had me sussed, though; he was shrewd enough to see that I needed more in my life than mundane things and that was probably why he used this as a tool to haggle down the price of the information that I had given him.

"Hi Carl, hope you've been keeping well," remarked Rashid as I opened the front door and let him in.

"Oh, so so, Rashid," I replied, not mentioning that Angela and I had been arguing about him only a short while earlier.

"So, let's get straight down to business, Rashid. What is this idea that you've had?"

"Well, I really do think that the way to go with biased wheels is to deliberately make them biased. This way it leaves no trace afterwards and any bias detection software will not pick up on it. Do you know any way that can create a bias?"

"Yeah, loads of ways, some practical and some not so practical."

"If a roulette wheel is not level, can that create a bias?"

"Definitely."

"If it is biased, how is it biased?"

"For a start, if a wheel isn't level, even by only a few millimetres, you get a down slope and an upslope." At this point I went into the kitchen and came back with a dinner plate to explain properly what I meant. "For the purposes of this example I will exaggerate somewhat so you get the drift. When the ball starts to slow down, the likelihood of it falling from the ball track will increase dramatically if the ball is on the 'upslope', because it is at this point that the ball is losing the most speed and energy." I tilted the plate to show the effect of what I was talking about. "When the ball is on the down slope and slowing down it will decrease in speed at a slower rate because it is picking up speed on the down slope. This means that the ball will likely fall from the ball track in the same section of the wheel because a wheel isn't level."

"So how do you know where the numbers are going to be when the ball drops?"

"That, my friend, is the sixty-four-thousand dollar question. You see we have three variables at work here. We need to know where the ball will be falling from the ball track, how long the ball will be airborne and the rotor speed."

"Can this be done?" inquired Rashid.

"Of course. I did it as a relatively inexperienced croupier with the naked eye and feel and hundreds of hours of practice. Although one advantage to doing it as a croupier is that you get to have the wheel going at whatever speed you want and not the punter. Anyway, what is this idea that you've regarding roulette wheels?"

"I had this idea about having a couple of really heavy guys or maybe just one single guy sitting near the wheel and putting all their weight on the table. Maybe even hide secret weights inside their clothing to increase the weight. The more weight on the table, the more uneven the wheel would be and the greater the bias… What do you think, Carl?"

I laughed out loud, which visibly upset Rashid, who asked:

"What's so funny?"

"Don't you think that stuff like this has not been tried before? It is far too blatant to work and they would be on to you in a flash."

"Even if they do, so what, we just do as we are told like good little boys and stop putting our weight on the table. You once said to me that staff are quick to tell punters not to lean or sit on the table. Well we won't be sitting or leaning on the table; we will just be sitting *at* the table, which is not a crime, is it?" insisted Rashid.

"I see your point, Rashid, but this seems too blatant to be workable to me. We don't even know if it would have an adequate effect, anyway. The wheels are very heavy and far heavier than a lot of people think. I think that it would need an awful lot of weight to have any kind of effect, so much so that the croupier or inspector would notice the table slanting."

"Yeah but would they be bothered to do anything about it even if they did spot it? I mean it's not their money is it? You told me that 90 per cent of them couldn't give a damn anyway. What I'm thinking is that we need more than your ordinary bog standard bias if these new Huxley wheels can be beaten," said Rashid.

"I see what you mean, but I'm still convinced that there will be some out there that are exhibiting some kind of bias; it is just a case of finding them, that's all. If I were you, Rashid, I would seriously think about forgetting all about this idea. If you get caught doing this you could get into serious hot water."

Rashid laughed out loud: "Carl, I've been in serious hot water most of my life; it's where the money is my friend."

As an afterthought this reminds me of an incident some years back where a guy got access to the casino after hours by hiding in the building. After everyone had gone home, he left his secret hiding place and did a little rearranging of the woodwork on one of the roulette tables. What he did was to cut a V-shaped wedge out of one of the legs of a roulette table and then loosely put the piece of wood back into the slot from which it came.

He went back to his hiding place and stayed there until the casino was busy and then subtly left the building. But his accomplices came in and approached the table where their friend had been busy during the night. Unknown to the gaming staff, one of these guys quietly kicked the loose V-shaped wedge from one of the legs, thus making the table uneven. Obviously when a roulette table is uneven the wheel is uneven as well. Only after the team had left the casino with very substantial amounts of money was the loose V-shaped piece of wood detected lying underneath the table.

This would be far more difficult to do now with CCTV and motion detectors, not to mention a night watchman, but not all casinos are this well protected. If I had been that way inclined, I could have hid in every casino that I've ever worked in and stayed there undetected after everyone had left, and I don't mean as a croupier either. I'm not talking about areas that are only accessible to staff. I'm talking about hiding places that any punter with the same idea could have hidden.

The last place where I worked had loose removable panels in the toilet ceiling. If you were fairly agile, all you had to do was go into a toilet cubicle and close the door behind you, stand on the toilet, gently push the ceiling panel upwards and pull yourself up and stay there. After the panel had been replaced into its slot no one would be any the wiser. I could have gained access to that casino after everyone had left and done whatever I wanted.

It would have been simple but I'm positive that this trick has been performed more than once around the world. The hardest part would be to get into the building, and this has already been done.

It has to be said that the people who executed the ploy with the V-shaped wedge still had to have the data regarding the rotor speeds and ball speeds to make it work. Even once you've narrowed it down to those two variables, it is still no mean feat to pull it off. One of the keys to the entire operation with ball drop-off prediction that does not involve biased wheels is to have a croupier who is relatively constant with their ball action.

Having a croupier who is constantly messing with the wheel speed and ball speed complicates the process immensely when you are attempting to do this without a computer. So the upshot of the meeting with Rashid was that I eventually talked him out of his idea, although I have to say that it could possibly have worked in theory – I have to concede that point. But I told him that it would be far more effective to have got someone on the inside to take care of that side of things if he could manage it, and I knew that would be well within his capabilities.

Victory Over the Huxleys

I didn't hear anything from Rashid for about six months and assumed that I probably had heard the last from him. The new year had come and gone, we were now into 2004 and my online poker career was going from strength to strength. Angela's fireplace business was also beginning to do very well, so things were definitely on the up for us both. The only cloud on the horizon concerned Angela's health, as she was diagnosed with rheumatoid arthritis in May 2002 and suffered substantial pain for a while.

One day I received a letter and it was obvious from the envelope that it was of a personal nature. This intrigued me immensely as I rarely get letters of this sort. To my surprise it was a brief note from Rashid. He informed me that he had been trying to contact me but my mobile phone was inactive. In fact I had changed mobile phones several weeks earlier and thus had a different number. I had totally overlooked the possibility that there could have been people who might want to contact me who only had my old mobile phone number.

Rashid said he had been desperately trying to make contact with me for about three weeks. He gave me a couple of contact numbers and asked me to call him as soon as possible. I had to let a couple of days go by before I could contact him as I went to Blankenburge in Belgium to help train a blackjack player in how to beat shuffling machines. He was kindly paying my expenses and agreed to put me up for a couple of nights. This was my first trip to Belgium and I found Blankenburg pretty and clean, unlike many of the industrial towns in England.

When I got back, I immediately telephoned Rashid, who seemed very surprised to hear from me. "I thought that you had moved away, Carl."

"I lost your number and I've changed mobiles since we last met. How have you been keeping?"

"I've been keeping very well, thanks. I have some data that I would like you to take a look at for me."

"How did I know that you were going to say that?"

"I need data on these numbers. There are about a thousand in total. When can I have the results back?"

"I can let you have the result by tomorrow." The truth was that I could have done it in a fraction of the time but I wanted Rashid to think that I was working harder for my money than I actually was. As it turned out, Rashid had been to Pakistan to see his family and friends and had only just got back. Once again I had absolutely no idea how he had come by these numbers and I certainly wasn't going to ask any questions, mainly because I knew what the answer would be.

This particular set of numbers was showing a bias towards a group of four numbers – 19, 4, 21 and 2. Each one was appearing at a rate that was almost double the frequency that it should have been. Rashid had to be getting inside assistance with this thing, there is just no way that he could be stumbling onto these numbers. He provides me with a list of numbers and suddenly there is a bias there. But what was puzzling me was that if he was being assisted by someone on the inside, why in heaven's name did he need me to verify the data?

The only possible explanation was that the person or persons who were supplying the numbers couldn't tell the difference between true bias or not. To be honest, most people can't and I include myself on that list. It is very difficult simply to look at a series of numbers and spot a bias without subjecting those numbers to mathematical processes.

So once again we had a bias and a fairly strong bias at that. But the real coup de grace was the fact that this bias was on a Huxley wheel and a Mark VII if I remember correctly, although time plays tricks. I telephoned Rashid with the news and once again he seemed delighted.

I remember thinking what a shame it was that I hadn't known him a few years back when I was into blackjack – we could have made a very good team. But I only go to casinos these days as a bit of fun; I get a perverted sense of pleasure just walking into the places now. It has got to a stage where I don't even care if they know who I am or not.

You could say that I'm guilty of burning my bridges and you would be 100 per cent correct. The kind of life that I had back then with the blackjack team (read *Princes of Darkness: The World of Highstakes Blackjack*) was different. I was a single man for much of the time. I really wouldn't like to be working the kind of hours again that I worked then as it would be grossly unfair on Angela. I would have liked to have her along as a team member because her bubbly personality and substantial assets would have caused a serious distraction for any dealer. Angela has the attractive looks and charm to make anyone feel at ease but she has her own business to run and could never find the time. She is the most important part of my life now and rightly so because she has done an awful lot for me over the years. But I still get tremendous satisfaction knowing that my knowledge even now is helping to take hundreds of thousands of dollars a year out of the casino industry and put it back into the pockets of the punters. You could call me a variation on Robin Hood, although unlike him I'm also doing it for my own personal gain.

A couple of weeks later I received a telephone call from Rashid with the news that he had won around £27,000 from a casino in London over the space of two weeks using several different players as cover. He asked me if I had any contacts in that particular casino, which I did not. When I asked him why, he told me that it was because one of the team members had received heat.

Apparently what had happened to him was entirely normal, especially in the casinos that I have worked in. Gaming managers were observing proceedings and one even came and stood at the end of the table and watched what was going on. This unnerved Rashid's accomplice and he left the table.

This was the last thing that he should have done as it just made it look as though something was amiss with the game. The first thing that any gaming manager would think was that this guy was dodgy and then they would start to look for the reason. Casinos are fully aware that biased wheels exist. Their weakness is that staff become complacent over time because they see the same punters placing the same action night after night. Familiarity breeds contempt and with it comes complacency. Suddenly the security procedures, which should be in place all the time, start to slip and this is when casinos are vulnerable. They only realise that something was wrong afterwards, when it is too late and they have been hit.

The culmination of this Rashid Khan story is that between 2003 and 2005 he was responsible for winning around £150,000 from casinos in the south of England and London. On top of that were his successful trips to Holland, France and Germany, where he won a further £45,000. But it was the money won in England that was the most remarkable in my book. This was because it merely confirmed what I had always suspected, that the supposedly random John Huxley wheels are anything but and are vulnerable to people with the money and the proper knowledge.

Rashid Khan left these shores in 2005 bound once again for his native Pakistan, to my knowledge, and has not returned. I know he will be hitting casinos in Asia if and when he gets the chance, because this kind of thing is in his blood, just as it is in mine. Before he left Rashid asked me to teach him how to beat blackjack games with shuffling machines as there are apparently a large number of automatic shufflers where he was going.

I quite often think about Rashid Khan when I have a quiet moment to myself and wonder what he is up to, as he has not been in touch. I would like to think that he is still active and doing what he does best… what a man!

CHAPTER 4

GENESIS

There have been numerous gadgets and much computer wizardry down the years to assist and help punters to try and predict where the ball is going to end up on roulette. But the real holy grail is to be able to do this visually with the naked eye and nothing else. This is what is known as "visual prediction" or "reading the spin". This is the El Dorado and the lost city of Atlantis all rolled into one.

It is shunned and derided by many as being impossible, especially on the John Huxley wheels. You already know my thoughts on this matter so I won't repeat them here. But I only have to say two words to people who doubt what I say... The Salmon!

Remember him from earlier in the book, the annoying man who won on roulette almost as he pleased for several years? This feat was on the John Huxley wheels and although they were the earlier models, they were being touted as random wheels even then.

Back in my trainee croupier days, I knew of several other dealers who could do almost anything with a roulette ball in terms of aiming it at a specific section of the wheel, though you could talk to many more croupiers who would argue that it couldn't be done. This just underlines how difficult ball control really is, when you have vast numbers of people who argue that it can't be done, who are spinning the damn ball forty hours a week.

The problem was achieving any kind or real consistency because I now know that each wheel acts differently from the next. You could roll the ball on one wheel at a certain speed with a certain rotor speed and then repeat this precisely on another wheel, but achieve a totally different result.

I had been practising my spinning for many months, but just when I thought that I had finally got it cracked, the exact opposite of what I was trying to do would happen repeatedly for several hours. I suspected that there had to be light at the end of the tunnel and one evening in 1991 proved this to be the case.

At that time, the casino where I worked had seven John Huxley wheels of an earlier model. They may have been Mark IVs but it is a long time ago and time plays tricks. But they also had another wheel that looked and acted totally different from the Huxley wheels. Once again I can't remember the maker's name on that wheel; in fact it may have been a much earlier Huxley model for all I know. The wheel in question was situated on American Roulette 6 and was only ever opened when the other seven wheels were in full use.

This wheel had much deeper number slots than the regular Huxley wheels – they must have been two to three times deeper. Wherever the ball dropped from the ball track it seemed to stay there. Because this wheel was always the last out of the eight to be opened, I rarely got the chance to practise on it. Tonight was different, though, as I had three separate stints on this wheel during the same evening. By the time I came to go on the table again, I knew exactly what I had to do to make the ball move exactly as I wanted.

I came back from my break and the pit boss was a nice Asian gentleman called Ify. He told me to go and take the dealer off AR6; he was losing heavily and had already done a couple of floats in. This was my big chance to try out what I thought I knew – if I couldn't do it on this wheel then I couldn't do it on any wheel. The game had become very heavy by the time I tapped the dealer on the shoulder to inform him that this would be his last spin before a new dealer.

Suddenly the entire job had changed from being a dull, re-petitive grind to a highly interesting and intellectual challenge. Despite the fact that the salary was very poor, I was starting to love it. The dealer finished paying out and I took his place. The table was full of Chinese punters, as it usually was on a Tuesday evening. Tuesday was the main night for the Chinese contingent as this was the night when the take-aways and restaurants closed.

They viewed me with suspicion, as punters do whenever they have been on a successful run with a certain dealer and that dealer is replaced. It is this suspicion or superstition or whatever of punters that enables a new dealer to kill the game. Many punters believe incorrectly that the game is crooked. Much of this suspicion is based around watching Western movies with under-the-table buttons and the like.

In reality, the casino does not need to cheat and would be very foolish to do so, as it has an insurmountable edge if the game is played on the level. Any new dealer who comes onto a big game and spins a few empty numbers is going to kill the ac-tion. In fact, if they had leprosy, they couldn't kill the game any faster.

So here I was on the game and ready to do my stuff; after a couple of minutes exchanging cash chips for colour I would be off and running. It took about half a dozen spins to remember the speed of the wheel that I had before and the ball speed. During this time I was hitting big numbers and keeping the Chinese happy. On the next spin, every single number on the table other than 1 and 34 had chips on them. I had the wheel at the perfect speed and the ball in the perfect position.

I had found that I could move the ball around the wheel about eight or nine numbers from where it had landed on the previous spin. I could move it round further if I held the ball for a fraction of a second after I picked it up before releasing it. This time I was deliberately aiming for number 1. This was a deliberate attempt to hit an empty number, only this time I was *expecting* to hit it. A couple of the punters threw me call bets, but my gaze was fixed on the wheel.

The ball dropped from the ball track and BINGO… "One Red Odd" I cried out loud. This was 36 to 1 against that ball going where I had aimed, but of course I could have hit it purely by chance. The Chinese punters took the loss in their stride as I knew they would. I changed their cash and chips for colour chips; the chipping machine was whirring away with the sheer volume of colour chips that I had scooped into it from the previous spin. I knew that I would have a problem on this spin as getting the ball back to number I would be difficult with the system that I knew.

Therefore I decided to do something that was unethical and contrary to the good will of the game. I decided to pause for a second or two before I released the ball. In roulette it is deemed courtesy to spin the ball from the last number, but to hell with courtesy, this was my experiment.

Luckily for me the Chinese contingent were so busy placing their bets that they didn't even notice me pausing before I spun the ball. This time I had the ball once again perfectly where I wanted it to be in order to get it very close to number 1. I felt a tremendous surge of excitement as I released the ball. Once again I was being deluged with call bets and bets that were tossed my way in order for me to place them. The inspector was having his work cut out to keep track of all the bets.

I wasn't looking into the wheel when the ball dropped, and shouldn't have been doing so anyway. But the cries of "double" told me all that I needed to know. I looked in the wheel and saw that little white Teflon ball sitting plum in number 1 once again. I placed the dolly on the only empty number on the entire table and proceeded to clear the layout.

"One more of those and that should kill this game," said Andy, who was my inspector for this game. Andy was a likeable kid in his mid to late twenties. He was a keen follower of cricket and we had numerous conversations about the game while doing our respective jobs. Suddenly the howls of joy and excitement from the Chinese were not as vocal as they had been a few minutes earlier. Andy was right, because just two minutes later, the game was dead. Once more I aimed for number 1… and *hit it!*

Not only had I tripled number 1 but I had tripled a number that I had deliberately been aiming for. As I stood there on the empty game, while Andy's attention was switched on to the other game that he had to watch, I was trying to work out what the odds were of hitting a number three times on the trot while intending to hit it.

I knew that the odds of hitting number 1 purely by chance on each individual spin were 1 in 37 or 36 to 1. The odds of hitting number 1 on each spin were 36 to 1 and that couldn't change. But this was different, as I had deliberately aimed for that number on three successive spins. This changes things dramatically. I had achieved something I had set out to do, so the odds of me doing this at the outset had to be 36 × 36 × 36. I used chips to help me arrive at the answer and was shocked to discover that the odds for this result were 46,656 to 1. This wasn't just some ordinary treble that you would witness at least once a shift somewhere in the pit.

There was always the possibility that this treble on number 1 had occurred at the precise moment that I was aiming for it. But the odds against that must be fantastic, in fact not being a mathematician I would hazard a guess that the odds would be that very same 46,656 to 1, although knowledgeable readers can feel free to contact me and correct me on this if it is wrong. In my mind I had just done something that had odds of nearly 47,000 to 1 against it happening and it had happened at precisely the time that I was expecting it to happen.

That was it for me, now I knew full well why this wheel was on American Roulette 6 and was the last table to be opened. In fact I was surprised that this wheel was even allowed in the building at all. Whenever we had a wheel switch, this wheel would always remain exactly where it was, situated on the one table that was always the last to be opened. This couldn't be coincidence and the management must have been aware of the vulnerabilities of this particular wheel.

The One and Only Mrs Ferris

My self-induced empty game on AR6 was short lived. No sooner had I finished calculating the odds for my wonder strike on number 1 than I was interrupted by "I hope that you are going to be kind to me young man and spin my numbers; if you do then you can come home with me."

I looked up to see the one and only Mrs Ferris, a likeable and extremely loud woman who was probably around seventy years of age. She was always dolled up to the nines with loads of jewellery and make up. A nice lady but annoying at times simply because she just never shut up. Whenever she came to gamble she didn't bet small and any croupier had the capacity to lose several floats to her within a very short space of time.

Suddenly a wicked thought entered my head. I was going to try to hit her numbers of which number 17 was her biggest. I think that she bet family birthdays or lucky numbers or something because she was betting the same numbers repeatedly. I knew that it wouldn't be long before I would be taken off for a break. The dealers who had been taking me off all night had just entered the staff room for their fifteen-minute break and I knew that when they came back I would be taken off.

So I decided to see exactly what I could do in those fifteen minutes. There was nobody else playing on the table at that stage so this would enable me to get a few spins in before I had to go. Mrs Ferris bought in for £30 to begin with and I passed her six stacks of orange colour chips. She was full of her usual banter about what she was going to do to me if I hit her numbers.

Her first sizeable wager was on number 17, with further big wagers on 8 and 29. The fact that these numbers were not adjacent to each other made hitting them far more difficult. But I didn't have to hit them to be successful. Even if I merely landed the ball within a few numbers either side, this would be success and would dramatically alter the normal odds of the game in my mind.

My first attempt was to try and hit number 8 because this was the easiest to try and hit from where the ball was situated. This was a right-handed table and the ball lay in number 21 from the previous spin. I knew that it would be more difficult to keep the ball in that area and try to hit 17, so I went for number 8. I spun the ball at my usual speed, which I had perfected, and I made sure that the wheel was at almost exactly the same speed as well.

The ball came to rest in number 36, just three numbers away from Mrs Ferris's big number 8.This was close but not close enough. I made a comment to her that I was trying really hard for her to win, for which she thanked me and reminded me that I was just the kind of ideal toy boy that she was looking for. Somehow I got the feeling that she wasn't joking, either.

The very next spin I tried to hit number 29. I paused a fraction of a second before I released the ball as hitting 29 from number 36 didn't fit my natural system. My confidence in hitting or at least getting very close to numbers on this wheel was escalating very rapidly. I was trying to hurry the game along because I was due for a break. In fact my actions caused a swift warning from Mrs Ferris to give her time to get her bets on as she didn't want to be rushed.

I just smiled and gave her a few more seconds to place some more bets. Within a minute or so the sexual innuendos from this seventy-something vixen had intensified as I was carefully placing the dolly on a big stack of her chips on number 29.

"Oh my word you wonderful, wonderful boy. Keep that up and I'll show you the inside of my bedroom," she cried out, and I bet she would have done as well.

Before I was taken off the table for a break, I hit her big numbers on two out of the next four spins. When I was tapped on the shoulder to indicate that it would be my final spin, there were howls of derision from Mrs Ferris: "As soon as I win a bit of money they go and change the dealer."

In fact her outburst wasn't without merit. It was standard practice for pit bosses to remove quickly dealers who were losing heavily. Was this practice bad form and un-professional...?

Of course it was! In this instance I was due for a break anyway but that fact didn't seem to appease Mrs Ferris.

This was a very pivotal day in my approach to and understanding of roulette. My experiences on that roulette table that evening convinced me that a dealer can definitely control the ball and nothing that anyone can say will ever convince me otherwise.

I Hope You Like Dealing Blackjack

We fast forward in time now to the winter of 1994. I had become disgruntled working in the casino in my home town and was hired as a croupier in a casino about forty miles away. I didn't really want to go but the prospect of better money enticed me and a couple of workmates to make the trip. I couldn't drive at the time – the only one of us who could drive was a guy called Chris.

The minute that I set foot inside this casino for my very first shift, there was something about the place that I didn't like. Maybe it was because I had been used to the much more laid-back atmosphere of the previous place but this casino had the discipline of an army camp by comparison. Any inspector who was caught chatting to a dealer about non-gaming matters was cautioned. If it continued they were sent to the manager's office and received a verbal warning.

I never once felt comfortable even in the staff room, and I hated the punters that they had there. Suddenly on that very first shift I realised that I had made a mistake coming here. I think that the other staff resented us because we were denying some of them overtime just by being there. By the end of the first week I was getting a bit sick of the place and there was a pit boss who I felt like punching every time I saw him. He was the kind of cocky smart ass that I loathed and he was constantly trying to be witty and funny, but he was about as funny as a rottweiler sinking its teeth into your backside. The only person who didn't know he wasn't funny was him. He was forever making snide remarks to the three of us and hiding behind the fact that he was a pit boss.

But I was to get my own back on this arse wipe in no uncertain manner. I didn't know what it was with these wheels, but they just didn't have the same level of bounce that the wheels at my previous casino had. They looked like the very same low profile John Huxley wheels that I had been using previously, but they were different. It didn't seem to matter how hard you spun the ball, you just couldn't get the ball to travel any more than about twenty revolutions. On the Huxley wheels back home that I had been used to, I could easily get thirty or even thirty-five revolutions of the wheel whenever I spun the ball. We were using the very same Teflon balls with an identical diameter, so the difference in revolutions had to be caused by the ball track.

By the end of the first week I had decided to try and work out the vagaries of the wheels there. I was struggling on a couple of them but there was one particular wheel that I seemed to have figured out on American Roulette 4, which was a left-handed wheel. I normally didn't have the same level of feel in my left hand as I did in my right, but there was something about this wheel that I liked.

I had been having tremendous success on it earlier in the week and was hitting blocks and spinning out of blocks quite easily. In the time that we had been there, the pit bosses had not put any of us onto any big game, despite the fact that all three of us could deal the pants off any other dealer there. It had annoyed us that they refused to take us on as inspectors as well.

What this meant was that although we were being paid more money than in our previous job, we had in fact suffered a demotion.

The pit bosses there seemed to trust their own dealers when it came to dealing the big action. Well, like I said, there was this one pit boss who was annoying me greatly. He had come on for the night shift and the afternoon pit boss had succeeded in having a very good result. I remember thinking how great it would be to lose a huge amount of money and wipe the smile off this guy's face.

On American Roulette 4 I had the perfect opportunity. The only punter on my table was a short guy around sixty years of age. He just sat there and placed his bet whenever he played and never said a word to anyone. He was playing £200 per spin and simply played one £100 chip on number 5 and another £100 chip on the 5–8 split. This meant that if I hit number 5 I would be paying him £5,200 (35 + 17 lots of £100 chips).

On this particular night, this gentleman came on to my table and bought in for £1,000. I knew that I could get the ball close to his numbers but would need a fair bit of luck to hit them, as it was such a small target.

I had the wheel going at just the right speed and I released the ball at what seemed the perfect speed for it to be in the tier numbers. The ball fell from the ball track straight into the tier section of the wheel and came to rest smack bang in number 5. There wasn't a murmur from the grey-haired gentleman as I announced "Five Red Odd" and placed the dolly on the number. He reacted exactly the same whether he won or lost.

I glanced over at the pit boss when I announced the number because I knew that he understood full well what this meant, as this guy always placed the same bet whenever he played. I calmly paid out the £5,200 all in £100 chips.

"Lets try to make it a double shall we?" I said cheekily to the grey-haired guy (never knew his name), knowing full well that Mr Arse Wipe Pit Boss could hear me. Literally thirty seconds later I was announcing "Five Red Odd" again, this time even louder. I glanced at the pit boss again and this time his face was a picture. Gone was the laughing, smiling, wise-cracking guy who we had a few minutes earlier and in his place was a man who could very easily commit murder at this moment in time, and I loved it.

There goes another £5,200 making over ten grand in total in the space of a couple of minutes. By now several other punters had come across to watch the action and a couple of other roulette tables had also dried. Suddenly all the eyes in the casino were watching to see if there would be a treble. I was getting a perverse sense of pleasure out of this and had to try very hard not to burst out laughing.

But I was still smiling and laughing and joking with the customers and deliberately overdoing it to wind up the man in the black jacket. I could see the staff room door opening and four members of staff returning from their fifteen-minute break. I knew that I was coming off this table whether it was my break or not, and that this would certainly be my last spin. I tried to get another spin in before that happened but failed, as several other punters bought in and delayed me from spinning up.

The tap on the shoulder told me all I needed to know. "Last spin before a new dealer," I announced to the table, and proceeded to spin the ball for the last time on this table. By now it seemed that all the action in the entire casino had ground to a halt and was watching this one spin on American Roulette 4. I knew with a couple of revolutions of the ball remaining that this was going to be close and I was not wrong.

The ball dropped just outside of the tier section but that

didn't worry me as I knew that the momentum of the wheel would take the ball inside the tier. The ball was bouncing around 16 and 24, which are neighbours of number 5. It seemed to be coming to rest inside number 24 and an incredibly near miss. But what must have been the last dregs of energy remaining in that moving ball enabled it somehow to flip over the fret and into number 5, where it finally came to rest.

I was so convinced that the ball had finally come to rest in number 24 that I almost called it and had to try hard to stifle opening my mouth to announce "Twenty-Four Black And Even". Suddenly the entire place erupted with what must have been one of the loudest cheers ever heard inside an English casino. "Five Red Odd," I announced, for the third time, amid cries of "Is that a treble on five?" from several surprised punters. But the electronic scoreboard at the end of the table confirmed the story as three big red fives sat up on that scoreboard in succession.

So another £5,200 was going to be winging its way across the table to our man with the grey hair. On top of that must have been about another £1,000 in total payouts as other punters were lumping on number 5 and coming along for the ride. I had done in about seventeen grand in the space of five minutes and knew full well that the night shift was going to struggle to claw that back.

I was loving it and this must have showed on my face, because when I eventually came off the table and went up to the pit boss to find out how long a break to take, he asked, "Did you find that funny?" in a menacing tone of voice. I asked him what he meant by his remark – he probably thought that just because he had a gaming manager at the side of him that I was going to crap myself and not say anything back. He didn't know Carl Sampson very well. Keeping my mouth shut has never been high on my list of qualities, irrespective of who I was talking too. I always spoke my mind, but doing that can get you into trouble in the gaming industry, and is not a recipe for promotion.

"Seemed to me like you were taking the piss, laughing and joking with the punters. Do you like it when you lose or something? Is it all one big laugh?" he barked out.

I was trying very hard to keep my composure and replied, "Not at all, what do you want me to do... ignore them when they talk to me?"

Without answering my question he quickly fired another at me: "When you hit 5 the first time, why the fuck did you not speed the wheel up?"

"Because there was no need to. I've been dealing this game for five years and I think I know how to deal roulette. At the end of the day, hitting bets and making payouts is the best form of advertising and we are in the entertainment industry after all, are we not?"

This statement infuriated him even more and is a classic example of why yours truly never got promoted to pit boss, despite being easily good enough to do the job. "Is that a fact?" he replied abruptly, "Well I hope you like dealing blackjack because you can do your entertaining on there from now on... go and take fifteen minutes."

By this time I was having a very hard job not to burst out laughing, but that would have caused a serious situation and I would certainly have ended up in the office being reprimanded.

That was far and away the most enjoyable seventeen grand I had ever had the responsibility of losing. When I think about that incident now, twelve years on, it still brings a smile to my face. But it does prove three very important things. First, that casinos can't stand losing; second, that they look badly on any dealer who loses money; and third, that roulette *is* highly vulnerable. Once again we have a situation where I was deliberately aiming for a number and hit it. You already are aware of the odds of doing that on three consecutive occasions. If I'm still not convincing you at this stage of the book that roulette is not only beatable but can literally be taken apart, then for heaven's sake put the book down and go and read something else.

The Spins That Never "Existed"

Sometime after that evening with Mrs Ferris I discovered that I was having very good success on another wheel. This time it was the right-handed table, which was American Roulette 8. This was a £1 table back then and was situated near the restaurant. This was the modern low profile wheel by John Huxley and was supposed to be as near to being random as was possible.

Back in those early days, I was stupid enough to think that possessing ability that altered the mathematics of the game could only be of use in beating punters. This is because many dealers prefer being on "no games" so they can stand around chatting with inspectors or practising their chip tricks.

I always practised my spinning whenever my game was empty. On this particular evening, my game was empty and the inspector was busy watching the other game and chipping up for the trainee dealer who was dealing that game. Not all of the tables had chipping machines and a game could easily get bogged down with heavy chip action if you were not careful.

While all this was going on I was merrily contenting myself with trying to work out the nuances of this particular wheel. I had been trying for several weeks but couldn't manage to attain any kind of consistent results. All that was about to change tonight. I stumbled across a rotor and ball speed that enabled me to spin sections of the wheel with relative ease.

To be able to do this you must have your wheel travelling relatively slowly, otherwise the extra speed will only make the ball bounce around more when it falls from the track. Having a fast wheel would go a long way to randomising the results totally and had to be avoided. I had my wheel going at about fifteen revolutions per minute, which is quite slow.

I was picking the ball up and holding it before releasing it for half a revolution and doing all kinds of things. It didn't matter, of course, because I had no game to worry about, but I was about to do something that would once again provide further proof of the vulnerability of roulette. I was aiming deliberately for number 8 and hit it *five* times in succession.

Most of the staff where I worked had encountered four-timers but a five-timer was an incredibly rare bird and this was the only time I have done one. But once again I was aiming for this number so this wasn't an accidental result. I was trying to work out the odds of hitting the same number on five consecutive occasions while aiming for it, but the number was too big for me to work out at the table. I knew that it was big though. When I got home later and put the figures $36 \times 36 \times 36 \times 36 \times 36$ into my calculator the resulting figure was 60,466,176.

The odds against what I had done were over 60 *million*-1. To put this figure into perspective, the odds of winning the national lottery are only 14 million-1. I had just done something that was four and a half times more difficult than winning the lottery.

The sad part to this story is that I could never again replicate that success on this wheel. It was moved the following week and placed on a left-sided table and I just couldn't get the same feel with my left hand. You have to bear in mind that a large part of roulette wheels are comprised of wood. I think that the ball tracks start to perform differently for whatever reason and this has the effect of changing the ball drop-off point and how long the ball is airborne for.

You may recall me saying in the previous section how I couldn't manage to propel the ball any more than 20 to 25 revolutions inside the casino, where I tripled number 5. The main reason for this is the differences in the texture of the ball, but the condition of the ball track plays a very important part as well. Quite often a set of ingredients come together almost like an alignment of certain planets and everything is ripe for a killing. But this state of nirvana does not always last very long as the criteria that went to make that particular wheel vulnerable at that particular time have vanished.

This is why the overwhelming majority of croupiers think that it is impossible to predict spin. Even renowned experts in this field have come to the same conclusion. But the experts don't possess all the available data – if they did their opinions would be very different.

You need to know that it is possible to predict spin, and that in itself is a serious obstacle to overcome. Many croupiers have tried for years to do this, failed, and then simply assumed that the task must be impossible. Conversely, many croupiers aren't interested in attempting to find out; they just turn up and do their job night after night.

What you have left are a small number of dealers who have believed that the spin is predictable and then attempted to get to the bottom of this. The crucial thing regarding these people was that they never stopped looking for the roulette equivalent of El Dorado and persevered, sometimes for year after year. I was one of those people; I don't credit myself with more intelligence than the others, merely more determination.

But that has always been my story, once I get my teeth into

something, I never let go. Blackjack and poker have been perhaps the two greatest passions in my life and I was highly successful in both those fields. Roulette was the same. I wanted to beat this game theoretically simply because too many people were telling me that it couldn't be done. During my time working on the other side of that table I've lost count of the number of occasions where my actions on a roulette table have dramatically altered the mathematics that are inherent within the game.

The Conspirators

In 1991, shortly before I was promoted to inspector, there was an afternoon shift that I will never forget. I was promoted to inspector very rapidly and at times the number of breaks that I would get on a night shift would start to get embarrassing. This was purely and simply because of the amount of money I was losing on the tables. At that time here was another dealer called Nigel who had a very similar ability to mine.

This is a strange scenario because the more experience you get in gaming, the more you seem to lose the ability to do what I've been harping on about. When all you do all night is stand on the end of the table and watch what is happening, the feeling that you had as a dealer simply leaves your fingers. You gain more knowledge but you lose out on that sense of feel, at least that was the case with me. That was until the day arrived when I learned the theory behind what I was doing.

Nigel and I would regularly have bets with each other on who could hit the most numbers or spin the most sections. Nigel was so sure of his ability and I was so sure of mine. At the beginning, though, neither of us was aware of the ability of the other. If we had been neither of us would have entered into having bets with each other because it would have been so futile.

Nigel was as good as I was when it came to aiming the ball, even though he had not been dealing the game all that long. He believed like I did that the odds of roulette could be significantly altered in certain circumstances, and set out to find what they were. It soon became apparent to me that Nigel had a similar level of ability as yours truly when it came to this area of the game.

As soon as we each discovered how good the other was at spinning sections on our respective wheels we stopped betting with each other. Nigel could attain a very high degree of accuracy on AR1 as could I on AR2. One evening we decided to try and lose the most that we could the following afternoon. It seemed like a fun thing to do at the time, a little entertainment to liven up the dull, repetitive grind of the job.

By sheer chance, that particular afternoon shift had several punters who had the capacity to hit the casino for significant amounts of money. Significant by their standards and not by those of most other casinos. Ours was a small casino and it certainly couldn't afford to be hit for a sum in excess of £20,000. For the first two hours of this shift, nothing much really happened and staff were going on regular breaks every thirty minutes or so. But this was just the calm before the storm and maelstrom that was to follow.

At about 4:15pm, just over two hours into the shift, three of our biggest roulette players entered the casino within the space of about ten minutes. Nigel and I were on the same break. When we entered the pit and saw who was in there, we looked at each other and knew what we would do. Even more so when the pit boss directed Nigel onto his beloved AR1 wheel and me onto my AR2.

We grinned at each other wickedly and I said to Nigel, "Let battle commence."

"May the force be with you, Luke."

The action was so big that we both only had to hit one number to do a float in and Nigel had lost his entire float while I was still preparing to spin up. When he placed his dolly on top of a pile of chips that looked like a replica of the Empire State Building, I almost burst out laughing. Whenever one of us announced the winning number louder than we normally did, it was just to let the other one of us know what the other had done.

What made the situation even better was that we had only just gone onto the tables and therefore couldn't easily be taken off for a while without it looking too blatant to the punters. I was getting off to a slow start in comparison with Nigel, who was hitting big numbers for fun on his table. I was landing the ball right on the button, but it kept bouncing away into some other section of the wheel.

Nigel was losing about five grand as far as I could tell, and I was actually winning a bit of money, which was even more annoying. Then within the space of a couple of minutes everything changed. A nice little Italian punter called Giove came to my table and started to bet big on his favourite number, which was 17. I took the gamble to try and hit number 17, which was nowhere near everyone else's chips, but if I could hit it, I could close the gap on Nigel.

Giove was betting in 25p chips so his action looked enormous. I had the ball and the wheel going perfectly to land it close to 17, and I went for it. The stack of chips on number 17 was almost at head height and was in serious danger of toppling over. The inspector told me to change the chips for £5 chips so that they didn't topple over. Before I had chance to do it, Giove barked at us to leave them as they were, as changing them would be unlucky. Thirty seconds later, to an enormous cry of "Hi-yah" from the Chinese contingent, I was placing the dolly very carefully on top of the massive number 17.

I announced "Seventeen Black and Odd" louder than I normally would. I glanced at Nigel and caught him looking across trying to see what I had hit. When he saw it his face lit up like a firework. Nigel had a punter who was betting very heavy on 28, 7 and 29, while I just had 17 to work on. It must have taken me a full five minutes to isolate the number, clear the layout and pay out. In this time Nigel had a couple of near misses and felt the need to tell me so as well.

Clearing the layout and paying Giove must have taken a full five minutes, and the Chinese contingent were buying in for bucketloads of colour each. The table resembled that of a New York skyline by the time I had spun the ball. Seconds later I was announcing "Seventeen Black Odd" even louder, which was coupled with a much louder "Hi-yah" from the Chinese.

I could see that Nigel was almost simultaneously putting his dolly on his very own "New Yorker", number 29. By this stage we were almost laughing our heads off, but we had to be careful that it didn't look as if we were laughing at the loss of money. I was trying to make it look like I was laughing along with the punters and so was Nigel.

Then for some unknown reason, the rhythm that I had previously had just suddenly vanished and I couldn't get anywhere near number 17, however hard I tried. But the Chinese were backing the tier section very heavily and I knew that I would have to change my target if I was going to catch Nigel up. He was hitting big number after big number and I had counted three new floats in the time that we had been on.

I eventually found a new rhythm and starting clocking tier number after tier number, much to the joy of the Chinese. I felt they were close to walking off my table at one stage, which would have handed a tremendous advantage to Nigel. Much to my annoyance, Giove accused me of going cold on him and switched to Nigel's table, which produced a massive grin from Nigel, just to wind me up.

My game was just getting heavier and heavier as the Chinese were placing more and more chips on each successful spin of tier. Once again I had a massive game in terms of chip action. You see, many croupiers would look at the amounts that were being paid out and would call that a small game. If I was down in London dealing a game with £50,000 per spin going down in action, and the punter was playing in £1,000 chips, to be honest it would bore me stiff.

I was regularly dealing roulette games where there would easily be 1,000 chips per spin on the layout and that's one monster game to deal, not to mention control. On top of that you had numerous call bets and courtesy bets to place, apart from keeping a close eye on everything that was happening. Many croupiers wouldn't have been able to handle a game of that magnitude. But at the casino where I worked we were used to that level of action on the 25p tables. If you could control and deal a game like that you could deal anything.

By the time that Nigel and I were taken off for a break he had lost £11,000 and I had lost £8,000 – a total of nineteen grand in the space of forty-five minutes, and all in 25p chips. Now that takes some doing. The dealers who were taking us off were undoing some of our "good" work by winning money, but they never got the chance to win much back as the games quickly died, which they often do when a new dealer comes on and starts hitting empty numbers.

In the relative peace and tranquillity of the staff room, me and Nigel just shook hands and burst out laughing. We were laughing so loud that we had to be careful of them hearing us in the pit.

"Did you see that double of mine on 17?"

"Oh that was class, man, sheer class, but what about my 29, 7, 28 and 7?"

"I was pissing myself when I saw your face. In fact the look on your face was funnier than seeing you put the dolly on the numbers."

"How much did you do in?"

"I think it was about eight grand give or take."

"Beat you buddy, I did in about eleven."

"Yeah but the day is young yet, we still have a few hours to do some damage."

"I wonder which one of us will be put onto blackjack?"

"I don't know, but it is certain to be one of us."

That proved to be just the case – it was yours truly who was banished to dealing blackjack for the next hour or so. Nigel had been sent to open up a new 50p table. This was double the denomination of the tables where we had lost the nineteen grand. If he got off to a flyer on this table, I would have almost no hope of catching him in our conspiratorial session of losing money.

But I was confident that Nigel didn't have the same level of feel on that left-handed table on American Roulette 3 as he had on AR1. I was hoping that they would start to win money not because I wanted the casino to win money but because I just wanted to win our little bet. Within about ten minutes, Nigel had a heavy game. The Chinese contingent who normally left around 6pm were hanging around. When they saw Nigel open up AR3 they flocked to that table like seagulls around fish.

I couldn't see what was happening properly as I had my back to the action on the blackjack table. Within about fifteen minutes, though, I heard the pit boss contact the duty manager to ask for a fill on that table. That meant that Nigel had lost yet another float... damn it!

It looked as if Nigel was going to win our wager now as I was dealing to deadbeats on my game and had no control anyway over the outcome of the game. A few minutes later I overheard a conversation between a senior inspector and the pit boss that told me that AR3 with Nigel on it was losing five grand. This put him about eight grand ahead of me in the race and time was running out.

By the time that it had got around to about 8pm, Nigel had been responsible for losing in the region of about £17,000 all by himself. I had seen no further action to speak of, so I was still stuck on my original figure of £8,000. I wasn't even sure that what Nigel did on AR3 was entirely intended, because this wasn't a wheel that he had told me that he could do well on. The lucky son of a bitch had fluked it, that I was certain.

But despite that wheel being on a left-handed table, I knew that I could do well on that wheel because it was the same wheel that I'd had tremendous success on before they switched it and gave it a different location a few nights previously.

I was sent for a break and I knew that AR3 was my destination when I came back. But as I said before, punters are wary of new dealers and I would be unable to win all the money back anyway. As I walked past AR3 on my way to the staff room, Nigel looked up and smiled. "It's all over bar the shouting, buddy," he said, meaning that in the fifty odd minutes of the shift we had remaining I was too far behind to catch him.

At ten past eight, I came out of the staff room to find a very sweet lady called Eve taking a seat on AR3. Eve had the capacity to win substantial amounts of money as she tended to bet in £5 chips. She also bet heavily on the first dozen and especially the centre column numbers of 2, 5, 8 and 11. Three of those numbers were in the tier section of the wheel (5, 8 and 11), which meant that if I could hit the tier section repeatedly, I would stand a great chance of hitting her big numbers.

Nigel had won a bit of money back and looked to be ending the shift losing about fifteen grand. This meant that I had to lose around seven grand in about forty-five minutes of dealing this game to equal him. By this time the afternoon pit boss had totally resigned himself to an absolute nightmare result on this afternoon shift and was sitting slumped on AR5.

I was directed onto AR3 and as I took Nigel off he said "Last chance saloon buddy".

"I'm going to beat you if it is the last thing that I do," I replied.

Eve was a lovely woman around sixty-five to seventy years of age and she was always polite enough to ask me about my wife and young daughter. I was going to try my heart out to lose to this woman, for her sake and for mine. I set the wheel going at just the right speed and Nigel's previous spin had set me up for a tier spin perfectly. I released the ball and felt very confident that the ball would drop into the tier section and trust to luck then if it hit her numbers.

I was disappointed to see the ball fall from the ball track well short of the tier section and had resigned myself to clearing the layout and taking Eve's £100 that she had on the table for that spin, when the ball found a beautiful resting place… number 2! Eve had £15 on the number and another £15 on the splits, making a payment of 156 chips, each chip being worth £5. The first payout was £780 less her original bet… I was on my way.

I knew that I couldn't rely on hitting number 2 all by itself because it was too isolated from any other number. The big miss on the tier section had upset me because what I had previously been doing on this wheel was no longer working, and I couldn't understand why. I needed to find a correction and fast. But if there is one thing that yours truly is good at, it is being adaptable.

My next spin immediately found the tier section but it hit number 16, which was not one of Eve's numbers. The next spin found tier again but this time it landed in 27... damn it! But in the blink of an eye I hit 8 and 11 on consecutive spins and suddenly Eve was playing table maximums with her winnings. Suddenly the wind was changing direction and I followed this with a slam dunk of a double on number 5.

The timing was perfect as Nigel was just coming out of the staff room as the ball had come to rest in number 5 and I gave a rather vociferous "Five Red Odd and a *Double*" as he walked by. We exchanged glances and smiles, and he gestured as if to ask me how much I had lost. I subtly showed him four fingers to indicate £4,000. He knew that I was close to equalling him and could do it as well on this game.

Suddenly my progress slowed and I was no longer hitting a succession of big numbers. I wasn't winning money as before but I was slowly giving Eve more money by hitting her splits. I asked the inspector what time it was and he told me that it was 8:45pm. I had ten minutes left before I was taken off and I was still about three grand away from overtaking Nigel.

Suddenly I was back in the groove and hitting 5 and 8 on consecutive spins. I did a quick calculation – I had lost exactly six grand since I had come on this table. This meant that I was only about £1,000 behind Nigel.

The time was now 8:50pm and the inspectors came out of the staff room to take the afternoon inspectors off. To my horror, one of the senior inspectors called Tony came to my table to take me off a full five minutes and three spins early. The new evening pit boss had obviously decided that he wasn't going to risk keeping me on that table for a further five minutes.

I announced last spin for a new dealer; the target was pretty obvious. I could equal Nigel by hitting 0, 2 and 11 and beat him if I hit 5 or 8. As 5, 8 and 11 were all in the space of six numbers, they presented a pretty obvious target. I was cursing the fact that I was being denied my extra two or three spins to catch Nigel. Did they not know about our little side bet and how important it was to us? I summoned up all my energy for one last gigantic effort and I could almost hear Nigel laughing on the table behind me. I released the ball perfectly and I knew that the ball would be dropping on my designated area.

"Let's see if you can go out with a bang, Carl," declared Eve.

To which I replied, "Hope so".

My eyes were glued to that little white Teflon ball as it slowly but surely began to lose velocity. It started to fall into my target tier numbers but to my horror the ball hit a canoe (ball deflector) as it dropped, and this took the ball to the other side of the wheel. I was now hoping for zero to come in, which would have got me a tie, but no such luck. The ball came to rest in number 12 and I placed the dolly on the empty number with all the enthusiasm of a guy on death row.

Eve interpreted this sickening blow to the stomach as me being genuinely disappointed at missing her numbers, but I had my own reasons, even though I did genuinely like her. When I met Nigel in the staff room I could tell that he knew that he had won by the look on my face.

"How close did you get?"

I put my thumb and forefinger about half an inch apart and merely said "That close."

"How close?"

"About a grand."

"As close as that?"

"Yeah, I reckon I would have done you but I was taken off five minutes early."

"I noticed, but those are the breaks, partner," said Nigel triumphantly.

"Come on, let's go and get a drink," I replied, and we trotted off to the pub to chat and have a laugh about what we had been doing on what had been the most remarkable shift I have ever worked.

Shelling Peas

Shifts and incidents like the ones mentioned were far from being isolated. The trick to achieving what I achieved was to believe in it in the first place and then to practise trying to do it without faltering.

There were many incidents where I deliberately aimed for a number and hit it three times in succession. Over almost ten years and thousands of shifts and an untold number of spins, the only ones that stick in my memory are the memorable ones.

Like the time that a popular punter and poker player called Shah came up to my table on AR4 and placed £15 on number 17. Shah was a very strong poker player by all accounts, and a very likeable guy. He was precisely the kind of guy who you liked to give money to. But like many good poker players, they don't touch roulette, or very rarely. Shah hardly placed a bet on roulette in my time there but this time he just ambled over to AR4 where I was killing time talking to the inspector on an empty game.

"Go on, Carl, let's see if you can give me a number," said Shah.

Thirty seconds later I was paying him £525 and luckily for him he decided to leave his bet on because I *tripled* it: £1,575 and it was like shelling peas to me at that stage of my career. In fact I wasn't all that far away from giving him a four-timer. This prompted Shah to say, "You are the *only* man to hit my number in twenty years." Right up until I finally left the casinos for good in 1998, we still talked about that three-timer on 17. But these incidents were common. Most of the time I was doing it to wipe out punters who I didn't like or simply because I was trying to kill the game for an easier shift.

There was the time that a certain female pit boss had really pissed me off and I went onto AR4 and gave twenty grand to a nice kid called Steve Utley in the space of twenty minutes by hitting his favourite 29 five times in seven spins. But having the ability to beat roulette is a bit like believing in UFOs. If you are one of the very tiny percentage of people who have seen one, the question of whether there is intelligent life in the universe other than ours has already been answered. It is the other unfortunate souls who must persevere trying to seek the truth. Like they say in *The X Files*, "The truth is out there!"

Chapter 5

The Mechanics of Manual Tracking

Much of what I've been harping on about in this book will be contained in this one chapter. Manual tracking, ball prediction or visual tracking, or whatever you want to call it, is the art of predicting where a roulette ball will end up. By sheer definition, manual tracking means precisely that, tracking a roulette ball with the naked eye and not by using a computer.

Despite not having the accuracy of a computer, visual tracking can and does substantially alter the mathematics of roulette. It also means that if a roulette ball can be tracked, any dealer has the capability to alter the mathematics of the game all by themselves. But in my experience, perhaps no more than one or two croupiers in a hundred have the capability to do it. Many think they can but they are simply fooled by results from a biased wheel or a statistical variance.

The reason why a particular dealer can be successful and others can't is easy to explain. Like I said earlier, most simply don't even try to find the answer. Some try for a short while and then give up, either because they fail or because they hear other croupiers tell them that the game is purely random. But if I had one hundred of the best roulette minds on the planet in front of me telling me that it is simply not possible to predict where a roulette ball will end up, especially on the modern wheels, I would tell them they are not in full possession of the facts.

I don't credit myself with any special gifts or intelligence. I found the answer simply because I persevered when few others did. To do this also takes an awful lot of concentration and sheer hard work, and most people don't like working hard. I found it very easy to work hard because of the enormous interest that I had in the subject. In fact I didn't even deem it to be working at all.

Although much of what I have to say would be very difficult to put into a book, anyone who is interested in taking this further can contact me through www.pokersharkpool.com. But what is essential for manual tracking is that certain criteria have to be met for it to work. The wheel head must be travelling relatively slowly. I used to have my wheel travelling at around 15 to 20 revolutions per minute. At these speeds, the ball is less likely to fall and hit the metal deflectors and bounce away.

Also, when the ball does make contact with a deflector and keeps it airborne for a fraction of a second longer than normal, the slow speed of the wheel head means that the predicted section can still be hit. With the new ultra-modern Huxley wheels, section betting is a very reliable and workable tactic. Many croupiers have fast wheels for reasons other than security. Sometimes it can be because the bearings in that particular wheel are making the wheel head slow at a rate that's faster than normal and dealers keep their wheel going fast in order to compensate for this.

What you are essentially looking for as a punter is a dealer who is careless with their wheel. By this I mean a dealer who is spinning the ball at the same pace and has their wheel revolving at relatively the same pace as well. This makes visual prediction easier but it is certainly far from being straightforward. Unless you happen to be using a computer, any dealer who constantly varies their ball speed and wheel head speed should be avoided.

Subtle Differences Can Be a Killer

Even for those who master this very difficult discipline, like The Salmon for instance, you can never really lower your guard. What we have here is a subject that's more complex than any other in the field of gambling in my opinion. Anyone who can achieve success in this way has the capability to beat any gambling game in the world that can be beaten by knowledge and skill. Playing winning poker and blackjack pale into insignificance by comparison in terms of difficulty.

For instance, the differences in ball textures can mean significant differences in performance and many dealers change their ball usage at regular intervals. This is the primary reason why casinos change balls. What reason could they possibly have other than that they know that roulette is vulnerable to prediction players? In the olden days of gaffed roulette balls and magnets I can understand why they needed to switch balls, but surely not today.

Another factor that complicates the prediction process is the amount of action and spin that's put on the ball by various croupiers. In fact the same dealer can put varying degrees of spin on a ball when launching it around the wheel… I know that I did. Sometimes through carelessness, I would get the spin all wrong and spin it without it being properly seated in the ball track. This causes the ball to vibrate as it spins or to fly out of the wheel entirely.

It always makes me chuckle when I hear so-called experts or croupiers pound on about how ball aiming is futile. The experts are basically taking notice of the croupiers who don't know any better. I've played blackjack and poker professionally, and the vast majority of players who play those games are losing players. Does this mean that the games cannot be beaten?

During the Second World War, the top scientists in Britain and America said that it was impossible for the Germans to have a long-range rocket programme that was anywhere near being operable. They were quoting ten to twenty years for the Germans to be in a position where they could hurt us from the confines of their own country. Shortly afterwards, large numbers of V1 rockets were sighted over the south coast heading for London, and the rest as they say is history.

This demonstrates something that's very important – that you can't just assume that an opinion or view is necessarily correct just because it is shared by large numbers of people. If we always took accepted knowledge and beliefs to be correct, how in heaven's name would the human race ever advance? We advance simply because of the tiny number of people who question those beliefs and seek to find answers and improvements.

Roulette is no different from any other subject in that respect. I hate it when someone tells me that something can't be done. Most of the time it is because they were not looking hard enough or looking at the problem from only one angle.

Another area that must be addressed on the subject of the amount of spin and action that the dealer puts on the ball is how many revolutions the ball makes around the bowl. If a dealer is only doing short spins, this can make the prediction more difficult and also presents the player with the problem of having less time to put their bets on. But there is another far more potentially serious problem to overcome. This is that the spin that each croupier puts on the ball takes a certain number of spins in order for it to dissipate. Tracking can really only be done once this action has disappeared and is a major reason why certain dealers have totally different results on different wheels. This was probably the reason why Nigel and I, although we had very similar skill levels when it came to aiming, achieved our success on different wheels.

The casinos take ball aiming and spin prediction very seriously indeed. It is why many casinos will not allow their wheels to fall under a certain speed. I once worked under a gaming manager and ex-general manager who was exceptionally paranoid about this. But he knew just like I did that roulette was a highly vulnerable game when the conditions were not optimal for the casino. The only trouble with him was that his paranoia slipped over into stupidity at times when he insisted on having the rotors going so fast that the ball would frequently bounce out of the wheel.

He also insisted on super-fast wheels simply because a table was losing money, which is ludicrous. In fact it was a common sight to see him walk up to a roulette wheel on a table that was losing money, put his hand into the wheel and speed the thing up manually, which is grossly unprofessional.

Another factor that aids any visual prediction system is the liveliness of the ball. A lively ball coupled with a fast wheel and a dealer who constantly deviates their spin randomises the result or makes it so difficult to predict that it may as well be random even if it isn't. This leaves the situation almost impossible to track except by computer.

Learning to Track

I will assume that the game is being dealt inside an English casino where the dealer does not reverse spin. Reverse spinning is the procedure carried out in many casinos to thwart visual trackers. The dealer alternates the direction of the wheel from spin to spin and also the direction of the ball from clockwise to anti-clockwise and vice versa. There is no reason for this tactic other than to try and randomise the result.

I would seriously recommend to any beginning tracker that dealers who reverse spin should be avoided or to only track the dealer when he is spinning the ball in the same direction. Tracking without a computer takes a very high degree of concentration and is certainly not a feat for the mentally idle. This tends to slip into blackjack territory, because one of the primary skills of successful tracking is to appear as if you are not concentrating on the wheel at all.

Any punter who stood next to a roulette wheel for thirty minutes without placing a bet and then placed a bet that was successful would be viewed with suspicion, even if that player was totally genuine. But there is information that you must find out in order to be able to track properly. You must find out the exact speed of the wheel in revolutions per minute and also the exact speed of the ball at certain points in its journey. The third and final criterion is to find where on the bowl the ball will drop, but this can be ascertained by finding out the ball velocity.

This is information that's too drawn out and complex to put into this book, and something that shouldn't be common knowledge anyway. However, I train people in this area and anyone who is interested is more than welcome to contact me. The Salmon had this down to a fine art on one particular wheel, although he still didn't know what I knew, or he could have been successful on other wheels as well. The following chapter describes my meeting with The Salmon and our conversation. We developed a mutual respect for each other after that, although we never became friends because we were too far apart as individuals and had nothing whatsoever in common other than roulette.

CHAPTER 6

MY MEETING WITH THE SALMON

This meeting took place in the autumn of 1994. I bumped into The Salmon on a shopping trip. I saw him before he saw me and I was debating for quite some time whether or not to go over to him and make myself known. I knew that he would recognise me instantly and may be afraid to talk about matters freely, especially if he thought that divulging anything to me may potentially cost him an awful lot of money.

It felt awkward to go across and speak to him because I hardly ever spoken to the guy when he had been only standing a few feet in front of me placing his bets for the past several years. To speak to him now would look odd. I quickly concluded that there was no way around this problem and I should either walk away and let the situation go or just ignore the awkwardness of it and dive in.

But there were things that I wanted to know. I was fairly confident that I knew what he was doing on roulette but I couldn't be certain that his methods of winning were the same as what I was doing on the other side of the table. After all, there was no real science to my techniques at that stage, I was literally doing everything by feel and so was Nigel. Nigel and I had often discussed this in private and we had agreed that we had an incredible feel for certain wheels in the pit. So I plucked up the courage to approach The Salmon.

"Hi, doing a bit of shopping," was all I could think of saying at the time.

"Oh hello. It's Carl, isn't it, from the casino?" He knew my name from the silly little name badges that we had to wear. I used to hate wearing them as certain punters that you didn't even like would insist on calling you by your first name.

"Yeah. Have you been down to the casino recently?"

"I went there last night and won a couple of hundred."

When most people say things like this you have to take it with a large pinch of salt, but this guy was different. In fact if he had said that he had lost a couple of hundred I would have been less inclined to believe him, given his history and the fact that I had been clocking him for so long. I sensed that he seemed very wary just talking to me because he knew that I always tried to make life difficult for him whenever he was on my table.

This meant that I could never make him believe that I was just being friendly because we would have easily just passed each other blatantly in the street – we both knew that. We made another series of meaningless sentences at each other and it was starting to get a bit awkward. I could sense that he wanted to call time on this little meeting.

"I think that I may have some information that may be of interest to you." I said this without thinking it through and I wasn't even sure if I had anything at all that would be of interest to him. But I also knew that he was ahead by as much as twenty grand over the time that I had been tracking him. That meant that if he knew that I knew that, he would assume that the casino knew it as well. This would be very valuable information to him, but of course the casino didn't know it as The Salmon was very clever to keep himself off their records.

"What kind of information?"

"About roulette, I know how much you are ahead this year."

He looked a little startled at first and then replied, "Go on then, how much?", with a disbelieving smile on his face.

I didn't answer the question but replied "If you continue then they will bar you." This was another lie but I had to get this guy's attention somehow. "Listen, do you fancy meeting for a drink and having a chat? I think that it may be in your best interests."

He looked at me for a few seconds with that "What's in it for him?" look on his face and said, "Yeah all right, I just have another couple of places to go to and then I'm free for a couple of hours. How about you?"

"I'm free all afternoon. How about we meet in the Mulberry at two for a pint?" I replied.

"The Mulberry?... Oh I know where that is. Yeah, go on then, see you there at two."

With that we parted company with me feeling good about myself that I had summoned up the courage to approach him in what was sure to be an uncomfortable situation to begin with. I knew that he was just as curious about me as I was about him. Numerous punters would love the opportunity to have a chat with a croupier away from work and get to know what they know. Most would be disappointed, however, because the vast majority of dealers don't know jack when it comes to ball aiming.

With that I went and did a bit more shopping and then killed a bit of time in the local library before heading for the pub. I got to the Mulberry at exactly 2pm and immediately scoured the place looking for The Salmon and couldn't see him anywhere. Suddenly the thought came into my head that he may have got cold feet and decided not to turn up.

These thoughts increased when it reached 2:15pm and he was still not there. Surely if he had no intention of meeting me he would have told me straight away? He knew full well that he would have to face me soon enough at work anyway, and this would have created another awkward situation. Just then the door swung open and in he walked with a couple of bags of shopping. He stood and scoured the pub for a couple of seconds before locating me.

We exchanged smiles and while he was at the bar getting himself a drink, I was mentally preparing what I was going to say. I had to give him a legitimate reason for being here and for being interested in him. He must be suspecting that I could be a casino mole trying to find out the truth. I could be one of those career-minded types for all he knew, who would be prepared to do anything in my own time in order to get promotion.

If only I could convince The Salmon of the truth, that this was light years away from what I was really like. I knew that I was going to have to lie to him to convince him that I was not a threat and that I really did have information that was useful to him. By this stage he had got his drink and came across to my table.

"Not very busy in here is it?"

"Never is at this time of day." I hated it whenever I made small talk with anyone when I knew full well that there was a hidden agenda, it always seemed so false. I quickly turned the conversation around to what we had both come here for. "Like I said earlier, I have some information that may be of use to you."

"You intrigued me when you said that, Carl, and that's the

only reason why I'm here, really," replied The Salmon. I realised that I still didn't know his name and I duly asked him before we continued with the conversation. He knew that I could have easily found out his name just by asking someone else who worked with me, and if I was a mole, this could easily be a lie, designed to make him think that I was on his side. This meant that he had no reason whatsoever to withhold his real name from me and he told me that his name was Paul. Obviously I can't divulge The Salmon's real name because that would be chronically unfair, but at least I can stop calling him The Salmon.

"Well Paul, they are on to you."

"What do you mean *on* to me?"

"Well, not so much on to you but more a case of them being aware that you seem to win regularly and now they are clocking you for the first time. You see, Paul, I already know that you are ahead over the last year or so, but I have not told anyone. I estimate that you are in front by about twenty grand and when someone plays as often as you then that's no fluke over that length of time."

Paul just sat there and didn't speak, apparently trying to comprehend what I had just said. I went on, "The reason why I know roughly how much you are ahead is because I've been tracking you personally over the past twelve months and before you say that this isn't normal, I have my own interests for tracking you, Paul. You see, I've known that you can read the spin for some time and I think that you are being clever by keeping your buy-ins off the spender sheets as well as your winnings off the cash outs. I know all about the other punter who gives you £5 chips to play with to prevent you from buying in. I don't know if that's deliberate or not, but the casino has not been on to you until now."

The casino was certainly not on to him but he would suspect

that this would be the truth based on the accuracy of my other information. "I think that you have a skill that very few others in the world possess, but I've noticed also that you only seem to do this on the same wheel. I've an intense fascination with roulette and how to beat the odds of the game; most of the croupiers and pit bosses think that what you and I do can't be done but they are wrong. I know that you are looking at me suspiciously but this meeting could hardly have been planned, could it, unless you are going to go down the avenue of thinking that the casino is having you followed, which would be stretching it a bit. I've wanted to talk to you for a long time, Paul, but I never seem to get the chance at work and I have to be careful talking to punters like this on the outside because it isn't allowed."

Paul continued to sit there and just take everything in that I was saying before he hit me with a barrage of questions:

"So why should I trust what you are saying? You could just be trying to find out the truth for all I know."

"You've seen me in the pit, Paul; you know that I'm not the company type. I couldn't care less if the casino wins or loses. In fact I love it when they lose big."

"Yeah I know, I've overheard conversations between certain members of staff and some obviously care about that aspect of the job and some don't... I know that you don't," replied Paul. He went on "I've been watching you as well, Carl, I know that you can do things with the wheel and the ball. I don't know what you do but you do whatever you are doing far too often for it to be chance in my opinion. I would just like you to confirm what I've always thought: can a croupier control the ball?"

"Well, that all depends on various factors, the main ones being the croupier and the conditions of the wheel. A small number of croupiers can control the ball and obviously some can do it more than others. Sometimes some dealers can make it look like they are doing something with the ball but in fact are just getting lucky purely and simply by chance. I don't like to brag about these things but I happen to be one of those croupiers who can control the ball to a certain extent."

"When you say to a certain extent, does that mean that you can't do it all the time?"

"Depending on the wheel, sometimes it is far more difficult, for instance I'm better with my right hand than my left."

"So let us say for instance that you wanted to hit a certain section or you wanted to spin out of a certain section, just how would you go about it?"

"Well it's not something that could be put easily into words. I go an awful lot by feel. I started off by experimenting with various wheels and using different ball speeds and wheel speeds and just sort of fell on certain combinations of things that worked."

"Have you ever been in collusion with a punter?" remarked Paul, looking directly at me and making me feel quite uncomfortable.

"No but I know croupiers who have."

"Seems to me that you are missing a golden opportunity, seems such a waste to have that talent and waste it on winning money for someone else or giving money to punters who are not going to give you a penny in return."

"Yeah, tell me about it. There's no point in colluding with you though, Paul, is there, because you do well enough on your own." We both laughed out loud at this remark but behind it lay the truth. I could tell that Paul still didn't feel entirely comfortable in my company but his fears appeared to be easing somewhat.

I went on, "You see, the casinos are very paranoid and security conscious about roulette and I set out to discover the reason for that fear. I've never believed that the game is impregnable like it is touted. I wanted further evidence to support my theories and this was why I started tracking your results, even though you were falling under their radar. Because you are the only punter to my knowledge who wins this consistently it took me a while to compile the data. This is why I know that you are ahead by about twenty grand over the past year."

The Salmon smiled and said, "Make it about thirty, Carl, I haven't always played in the same club."

Here was a man telling me the absolute truth about what he had been doing on roulette over the past year. This wasn't some problem gambler type bullshit to appease his wife or to look good to his friends or all of the other fairy tales that I've heard from gamblers down the years to help to disguise losses. I knew that he could beat the game and Paul knew that I knew, but I just wanted to hear him say it for myself. This was just one more confirmation of the vulnerability of the game – as if someone like me really needed any more proof.

"How did you come about knowing what to do then?"

"Well I was like you really, the correct way to go sort of just appeared to me, but I've refined it over the years. I don't just win on the same wheel, you know, it is just that this wheel seems to be the easiest one for me to win on. When I tried playing on other wheels, I found that I couldn't replicate the same level of success for whatever reason. There were times when I was doing nothing more than recycle money because I was losing money back on other wheels that I had won earlier."

"When you say that you refined it over time, what do you mean?"

"Well, I first started to compile wheel speeds. I found that I could easily time the wheel in revolutions per minute by simply timing it between two fixed points with my digital stop watch. I soon became very good at instinctively knowing how many revolutions per minute the wheel was travelling. But my real breakthrough was when I came up with the idea of how to track the ball in relation to the wheel when it was travelling at various speeds."

I sat there mesmerised for a full thirty minutes and listened to The Salmon's theory of how he could predict when a ball was going to land by first identifying the moment when the wheel and the ball that were travelling in opposite directions were travelling at the very same speed as each other. Whenever the wheel head and the ball were travelling at the same speed after the ball had de-accelerated, you could in fact measure for how much longer the ball would be airborne and where it would land.

The Salmon showed me the mechanics behind what he did, but he still insisted that what he was doing was by sheer feel because translating the data and the tables of various wheel and ball speeds was just too long and cumbersome to do without the assistance of some sort of computer, and he confessed to not being computer literate. Paul's descriptions and analysis seemed to fit what I had been doing instinctively. He knew as well as I did that a ball could be tracked around a wheel and its path and exit points could be calculated by someone of average intelligence who had the foresight to look beyond what seemed obvious.

I asked Paul why he bet on only a couple of numbers or sometimes only one number whenever he placed a bet. He said that this was partly because he didn't have time to place any more bets and partly because he thought that betting on more

numbers was counter-productive. The way he viewed it, rightly
or wrongly, when he had formed his opinion of where the ball
was destined, betting more numbers was simply straying away
from his target area and so was futile.

To me, this argument had a certain element of merit attached
to it, not to mention commonsense. I was perfectly aware because I had done my homework that there had been many studies in the 1970s that were aimed at proving that roulette could
be beaten by visual prediction. Many of them argued that a
computer was essential in order to make this work. In my opinion they were important but far from essential.

Here I was in the mid-1990s and I knew several people who
could transform the outcome of roulette by either ball-aiming or
visual prediction, and these people were executing their skills
on the much superior John Huxley wheels. Casinos have always
strived to keep under wraps wins attained by visual prediction.
They know that it can be done, but the only wins that they want
published are those where punters simply got lucky. Prediction
players have been hitting the casinos now for over a hundred
years and they continue to do it, but only the ones who hit the
casinos for huge sums of money get noticed. Like those in the
early 1980s who hit numerous casinos in England.

But that's the tip of the iceberg, in the sane way that the Billy
Walters' case was to biased wheel play in the 1980s. I would like
to know what the real figure is for people like "The Salmon",
who have the skill but don't bet big enough to get noticed. Not
to mention the dealers who have the skill when it comes to ball
aiming. Based on my experience, I would say that at least 10 per
cent of croupiers have some sort of ball aiming ability.

But whether these croupiers could achieve results that were
consistent enough to overcome the house edge if they were
colluding with a punter is another matter. There are around 5
per cent of croupiers who have taken this skill further and can

cent of croupiers who have taken this skill further and can dras-tically alter the natural outcome of the game, but only chose to exercise that skill to beat punters.

Then we have people like Nigel and me, croupiers who have worked tirelessly on the game and practised their skills when others have got bored of trying. I mean, how many croupiers have the knowledge of roulette and the drive to find out information that's only for the ears of gaming managers like I've done? Not one in a hundred croupiers have my knowledge of the game, not to mention my contacts. Yet these are the same croupiers that the so-called experts talk to whenever they com-pile their data for some of these independent studies.

It was now Paul's turn to sit and listen to me while I gave him a history lesson in roulette and told him things that were simply top secret in the world of gaming. Like how the casinos in England were so scared of visual prediction and biased wheel players that they got John Huxley Ltd of London, one of the premier manufacturers of roulette wheels, to attempt to design a wheel that was totally random. This led to the creation of the new low-profile wheels but the casinos are seriously misguided if they thought that these wheels prevented people like The Salmon from beating them or dealers like me from influencing the game

But the overwhelming success of these new Huxley wheels was in the fact that beating the game by biased wheel play and visual prediction suddenly got a whole lot harder. There is no doubt that many people who were beating roulette by either of these two methods would have been put "out of business" by the sheer quality of the early Mark IV's for instance.

What these new low-profile wheels did was enable even a novice dealer to randomise the game almost totally, to an extent that a highly successful computerised prediction system couldn't overcome the house edge. But the weakness of these wheels still lies in the fact that they are not used and maintained properly. I don't believe that even the ultra-modern wheels of today can be totally random without some sort of dealer assistance. This is because if the wheel is travelling beyond a certain speed and the ball is bouncing around too much, predicting where the ball will drop is still next to useless information.

There was no doubt that I had information regarding roulette that other croupiers who I worked with simply didn't have, but being very good friends with certain gaming managers and pit bosses does have its advantages.

"So, Carl, does the ball make a difference? I've noticed that you keep a spare ball in the groove at the top of the spindle and the composition of that ball is not always the same."

"Yes, the ball design certainly does make a difference although the difference in composition from ball to ball is nothing sinister in this casino, they just have a selection of balls that they use, that's all."

"I've noticed that there's a ball that's whiter and larger than the others that doesn't seem to bounce around as much, and that I win more when this ball is being used."

"Yeah, it's made from a substance called Teflon and it is by far the best ball to track because of its lack of bounce. In fact many casinos refuse to use these balls full stop, preferring the more energetic nylon and acetal balls."

(As an add-on to this topic, one of the casinos where I subsequently worked did indeed keep a different composition ball on the table, which would be subtly switched into play if ever the table was losing in a certain manner. They were only too well aware of visual prediction bettors and the vulnerability of roulette.)

"Do you like the Teflon ball better when you are aiming?"

"Yeah, it's miles better than anything else."

"Would you like me to let you into a little secret?" asked Paul, with a rather cheeky grin on his face.

"What's that?"

"Me and a couple of my mates look to see if you are on a big game with sizeable chip action. We know that you will be aiming away from the big numbers and bet on the empty ones on the other side of the wheel. We have cleaned up loads of times doing that," remarked Paul.

I laughed and said, "You had better be careful doing that because I'm not always trying to miss their numbers. If I like the punters, I'll be doing just the opposite, or if I'm trying to get an early break then I'll try and hit the big numbers."

"I'll remember that. I don't suppose you could give me the nod next time, could you Carl, and let me know which way you are going?" inquired Paul, with yet another cheeky grin on his face.

"No problem. You said that you go an awful lot on feel, Paul, but do you look for certain characteristics in dealers as well?"

"Oh definitely. I hate it whenever they start messing around with the wheel and speeding the bloody thing up so that you can barely see the numbers. Sometimes the inspector even puts their hand into the wheel and speeds it up for them. Are they supposed to do that?"

"No, but it is only bad etiquette, that's all. There's no law that says that they can't. I've always been meaning to ask you why you haven't started playing for more money, although I think that if you did, you wouldn't last very long."

"You've just answered your own question. If I played for

bigger stakes, dealers would start to mess around with the wheel the moment that I walked up to the table, wouldn't they?"

I simply nodded in agreement and refrained from telling him that I would have done the same.

"You see, Carl, I earned thirty grand last year from doing this and this has prevented me from having to work. If I increase my action I could jeopardise the entire thing. In fact you are the only person who knows that I win consistently. I haven't even told my friends what I know and my parents don't even know that I frequent these places. So you see that I have an awful lot to lose by increasing the action. At least this way I go undetected. But you said that you had heard things being said about me."

Then I realised that I had made up this story to approach The Salmon and now I had better think up some bullshit quickly because he was expecting an answer.

"It was just that I overheard a couple of pit bosses talking about what a lucky son of a bitch you were and that you always seemed to win. You may need to just be a bit more careful, that's all." Now that I'd had my suspicions about The Salmon's success confirmed, and had learned that he was doing even better than I had first thought, I didn't want my relentless quest to further my knowledge to interfere with another man's income.

"Well in that case, I'll take a few precautions, but I'm very glad that you've told me that Carl… Thankyou."

I looked at my watch and saw that it was 5:30pm. I had been talking to Paul for over three hours and I was on a night shift later on. Not to mention that my wife would be wondering where the hell I was. We ended the conversation and agreed to meet again in the future but never did. I left this particular casino in 1994 and never went back, and I left gaming for good in

1998. I quite often find myself thinking about The Salmon and wonder how he is doing and whether he is still active, or if the electronic wheels have put an end to his career.

What that meeting with The Salmon did for me was to make me realise for the very first time that I was in the right business but on the wrong side. This guy was earning thirty grand a year tax free and part-time. My main problem was the fact that even once I had left the gaming industry, I would still be pegged as an ex-croupier and watched like a hawk – and that was presuming that they even let me through the door. But as the saying goes, there is more than one way to skin a cat.

CHAPTER 7

THE MONTGOMERY MARVELS

Earlier in the book, I spoke about the remarkable exploits of Philip and Peter Montgomery, a couple of roulette mechanics who amassed over £250,000 from the game between 1999 and 2004. They made this money using a combination of past posting and stealing chips. Philip and Peter are their true first names but "Montgomery" is an alias, as once again I would prefer that their identity be kept a secret.

I first became aware of Peter Montgomery in the summer of 1998, just a few weeks before I was due to leave the gaming industry and commence my a career as a financial consultant. I was standing inspecting blackjack and Caribbean stud poker when I saw what appeared to be a very slick past posting move on American Roulette 2, which was just a few feet in front of me.

By this time in my career I had become so disillusioned with gaming that I couldn't care less if anyone was cheating or not. I had got into several arguments with gaming managers simply because I was no longer willing to keep my mouth shut whenever I didn't agree with something. I couldn't wait to get out of the door for good and I knew that the feeling from the management was mutual. A few months previous and I would have alerted the pit boss to what was going on but not now. I mean, there I was seeing something going off over on a table that I shouldn't even have been watching anyway.

I had been treated badly too many times to care any longer and the guy could have emptied the chip tray for all I cared. But his movements intrigued me and I carefully observed him while making it look as if I was watching my own games as well. But I wasn't watching my own games in the slightest, a fact that was made blatantly obvious when a player on blackjack claimed that the dealer hadn't paid him from the previous round of play. I didn't know if the dealer had paid him or not, so I just instructed the dealer to pay the man anyway to avoid any fuss and allow me to do what I had been doing... watching this slick operator over on roulette.

I had noticed that the dealer on roulette had only paid the guy £35. This told me that he had somehow slipped a £1 chip onto the number after the ball had dropped. He had past posted right under the nose of the dealer, who was very experienced, and the inspector, who was perhaps the most experienced at the club. At first I just passed it off as a one-off, a one time move by an opportunist that came off.

But in the next forty-five minutes, this guy pulled the same move another four times. If you took away his losing bets, he had made about £100 in less than an hour playing no more than £1 chips. This is where many past posters go horribly wrong. They waltz into a casino as total strangers and are not smart enough to realise that they stand out like a sore thumb to the gaming staff and management, who are actually expecting them to make a move.

This guy was known to all of the staff although I didn't know his name at that time. But his bets and action made him small fry in our eyes, someone who wasn't a threat and could never be a threat based on his action across the table. This guy's moves were very slick and accomplished and he operated totally on his own, or at least he appeared to. Over the next week or so, I kept a very close eye on this guy and learned that his name was Peter.

I learned something else as well – that he wasn't working on his own at all, despite what I had first thought. He was operating with a guy who came in several nights a week with another group of punters. One evening he was on my table for the very first time; I came back from a break and was told to take the inspector off AR3 and AR4 for a break. My pulse quickened when I saw Peter because I knew that he would try and make a move on my table and I wasn't sure what I wanted to do about it.

Should I leave it and let it go because I would soon be leaving or pull the guy and have him barred? I had a massive advantage over him because I knew what he was doing but he didn't know that I knew. Therefore I could easily entice him into making a cheating move by pretending to be distracted elsewhere and then confront him with his play. We had CCTV at that time as well, which would have easily backed me up in my case.

But I was intrigued more than anything else at what these two guys were doing. There was a Greek punter who kept coming down from the card room periodically and placing a £25 chip on high numbers. The table was very busy, as it usually was after midnight on a Friday. There was a guy who didn't appear to be with Peter who was persistently placing late bets on losing numbers. He had been doing this for several weeks and the staff had tagged the man as a bit of an ass. But there was something that didn't feel right about these two; my radar is a very sensitive one when it comes to spotting subtle tells and it was beginning to tell me that something was amiss here.

I had learned that this late bettor's name was Philip because I had overheard one of the female members of the party call him by that name. But what struck me as strange was that whenever this guy made a late bet with a 25p colour chip, the only person that didn't glance at him was Peter which I found to be odd. When somebody does something noticeable like Philip was doing, it is a totally natural reaction to look at them.

On one particular spin, the Greek guy came down from the card room and placed another £25 chip on high numbers. I acted as if I wasn't really paying that much attention and was constantly engaging the dealer on AR4 in conversation. Philip was standing with a couple of friends opposite the dealer while Peter was standing behind another couple of punters at the bottom corner of the table near high numbers. The table was bustling and the ball had already come to rest in number 9 when Philip as placed his usual late bet on number 27.

When he straightened up, the £25 chip on high numbers had gone. I was certain that Peter had taken it and a closer inspection through the CCTV footage in the office would have proved it without a doubt. But what these guys were doing was subtle: they were not placing late bets in the traditional sense but stealing bets that had already lost. They knew that it was far less likely to be picked up as the punter who had placed the bet simply looked and then heard the dealer announce "Nine Red and Odd", indicating that his bet had lost. He never even bothered to come down from the card room.

Also, waiting until the bet was lost eliminated the chance that the player came back to the table having changed his mind about the bet or to change it. A few spins later and the same thing happened again. I feigned a lack of concentration, they made their move and another £25 was theirs. I had to admire these guys, they had carefully selected their target and their moment, and their timing was spot on. I started to wonder how long they had been doing this little scam. Not once did Philip or

Peter even glance in the direction of me or the dealer, which cheats tended to do out of nervousness. This was always a prime tell that something was going down as there was no reason for a punter to be watching an inspector when they should be betting. Little did they realise that I had been setting them up to make the move. They would have been absolutely stunned to realise that I was doing this. I was faintly amused by the whole scenario and the professionalism and expert timing that they were employing.

Another factor in these guys being successful was the fact that they were only taking small amounts, which wouldn't alarm the casino. But they had just taken £50 in a matter of fifteen minutes, and that was not small change if compounded over a year. They didn't even care that the game was on CCTV – although most punters know that the CCTV footage only gets checked in the event of an incident anyway, and then only for serious amounts.

These guys were not claiming anything but this was a different tactic from what they had been doing earlier when I saw Peter past post a chip on another roulette table. After the second losing bet on high numbers, the Greek guy appeared to stop placing any more bets. Now I expected them to past post something on third dozen, probably a £1 chip. Philip had bought in for £25 of colour chips and the colour of those chips was purple.

Suddenly something occurred to me: Philip's colour chips were roughly the same colour as the £1 cash chips. It was all starting to fit into place. A few minutes earlier I had seen what I thought was hand contact between Philip and Peter at the bottom of the table, when Philip was placing a bet on third dozen. Now I wondered if Philip had passed some of his colour chips to Peter to assist him in making a move. I casually and carefully counted the purple colour chips that Philip had in front of him –

he had four full stacks of twenty and five chips on the top making eight-five chips in total.

With the three chips that he had on the layout, this made a total of eighty-eight chips. There were exactly nine stacks of chips per colour on the table with twenty chips per stack. I discreetly counted the purple chips inside the chipping machine and the purple chips that were also in front of the dealer and came up with a figure that was six chips short of what there should have been. There were definitely nine entire stacks of purple chips. Even accounting for the possibility that one or two had somehow got inside the chipping machine, we were still several purple chips short.

Now I was convinced that Philip had passed about half a dozen purple chips to Peter, who by this stage had bought in for several stacks of colour chips of his own. But the clever thing about what Peter did was that the colour that he bought in for was orange. In my mind he had done this for a reason, because he had specifically asked for that colour and Philip had asked for purple. The dealer completed the payout procedure and began to prepare for the next spin. I glanced at Peter and Philip and they looked entirely normal.

I was starting to like these guys, what really gets on my nerves are the blatant opportunists who think that they are really clever but are so transparent that they almost insult your intelligence. But these guys' movements and time misdirection was a joy to behold and would certainly have worked against a lesser inspector than me. Some people have a sixth sense; I sometimes think that I have a seventh and an eighth.

The ball fell from the ball track and was bouncing around before it looked likely that it would come to rest in either 1 or 33. Philip once again placed losing chips on numbers that were totally on the opposite side of the wheel. He obscured my view for a fraction of a second of the third dozen areas; when he straightened up, there was a purple chip with a £1 chip underneath it on number 33, just as I had expected.

While he had obscured my view Peter had slipped a £1 chip onto the number underneath. The dealer isolated the number and then made the payout, but nobody claimed the £35 from the single on number 33. I looked for Peter but he had walked away and gone on to another table. Could it be that he had forgot about the £1 chip? The dealer asked me what he should do and I instructed him to put the money on the wheel, as we did with any unclaimed bet.

Philip, who was playing in the purple chips, took his 35 to 1 payout in colour chips but made no move to claim the bet. I deliberately asked him if it was his bet in order to provoke a reaction, but he just stonewalled me by declaring that he wasn't betting in singles, which he wasn't. Now I was starting to doubt that Peter had placed the bet, as Philip wasn't claiming it and Peter had walked away. But just as the dealer was getting ready to spin up, Peter came back to the table and asked vaguely which number had won. He didn't direct his question to anyone in particular.

I asked him if he had £1 on 33 and he said yes. Then I instructed the dealer to give Peter the winning £35, and he gave one of the best surprised and startled looks that I've ever seen. I chuckled to myself because the guy was acting his heart out and was well deserving of an Oscar. The move was brilliant in its simplicity: he had walked away from the table without any apparent care in the world and not even tried to claim the bet. He had waited for either me or the dealer to ask whose bet it was before declaring that it was his.

Peter's entire act suggested that he didn't really give a damn about the £35 but seeing as it had won, he might as well take the money. Damn if I didn't like these guys' style; they were good. Nobody would care about £35 and a £1 chip on a number wouldn't alarm any of the casino personnel, and they knew it as well. A part of me wanted to rumble them out of personal pride, but what the hell? I was leaving soon and good luck to them.

In the short time that I had been clocking Philip and Peter, I had calculated that they had successfully claimed over £1000 in little more than a week, on numerous bets on tables that were being supervised by pit bosses. These guys didn't care who was watching the table – experienced inspectors, pit bosses or managers. In fact the more black jackets that were hovering around the table, the more moves they seemed to pull off. Of course the best time to make a move of this kind is precisely when it isn't expected. The element of surprise is always paramount with moves like these and the psychological prowess of what these guys were doing left an indelible mark on me.

For the next few weeks, I watched Peter and Philip pull off a wide array of moves on my table but more often on other tables without ever approaching them or dropping them in it with my superiors. Suddenly I was having dreams of training up arsenals of blackjack and roulette mechanics to hit back at the industry that had treated me so badly. This was back in the days before my first professional blackjack team. But even when I was in full swing with that very first team between 1998 and 2002, I was still being pestered with offers to hit the casinos where they could be hurt the most… on roulette.

CHAPTER 8

FANCY SEEING YOU HERE

I can remember the date exactly when I met Peter Montgomery in person for the very first time, and what an incredible fluke it was. The gaming industry and my role as a croupier were long since behind me and so was professional blackjack. I was earning a living now playing poker on the internet and this was providing me with an income that was above anything that I had ever had before. It was 30 December 2004 and I was up in Scotland for the new year celebrations, staying in a hotel called Montgreenan, which is situated about thirty miles or so south of Glasgow.

This plush country house hotel set in its own grounds was a perfect place to spend the new year with my partner Angela. If there is one thing about the Scots, they sure do know how to celebrate New Year's Eve. It was about 7pm and we were making our way down the rather grand staircase for dinner when someone caught my eye in the reception area. I have an excellent memory for faces – once I see a face I never forget it even though I can't always remember where I know the face from. I was unusually quiet all through dinner, and this must have been obvious to Angela because she asked me if anything was the matter.

"I have just seen a guy on reception who I know from somewhere and I can't figure out where for the life of me."

"Maybe it was from when you worked inside the casinos. After all you know thousands of people from back then."

There was one thing about Angela, she always had this unbelievable ability to put her finger right on it. Suddenly it hit me like a bolt of lightening: the guy on reception was Peter the roulette mechanic from my final year in gaming. It was six years since I had last seen him, but now I remembered him fully. The coincidence was amazing, meeting up with the guy inside a hotel over Christmas, in Scotland of all places.

Although it was like Angela said, I knew that many faces from my time in gaming that maybe it wasn't such a coincidence at all. This wasn't the first time that I had bumped into punters in places far from home. During my time with Steve and the boys in my first blackjack team, I had begun training players in how to beat roulette and I have to admit that some of those techniques came from stuff that I had observed from Peter and Philip.

After dinner I left Angela with a lovely Scottish lady at the bar chatting away about girlie things and went to try and find Peter, but without success. I was hoping that he had not checked out, because I dearly wanted to meet the guy and have a chat with him about what he was doing now and if he and Philip had been caught yet. I politely enquired at reception if Peter had checked out and was informed that he was here for another four days... my chance would surely come.

The following evening my opportunity arose as Angela and I were heading down to dinner. As we sat in a room adjoining the restaurant enjoying a drink, in walked Peter with a lady who was either his wife or partner, presumably, and they sat directly in front of us.

I gave it about five minutes – obviously I didn't want to jump on the guy immediately after he entered the room. I casually enquired if he came from my area and if he had ever been to the casinos there and he seemed very startled to be recognised so far from home. As it turned out, his wife was Scottish and her family lived outside Troon, which was just up the road, and they were meeting up here for the New Year's Eve party... small world, I thought.

After Peter recovered from his initial shock of being recognised, we agreed to meet in the bar afterwards. It is always awkward approaching punters outside a casino environment, especially when they happen to be with other people, because many of them are reticent about being approached and identified as gamblers. But of course Peter wasn't a gambler.

Peter was no more a gambler than I was. The term gambler has always been used very incorrectly and seems to suggest to many people a person who loses money that they can hardly afford, and who has some kind of a problem. This has long been a personal gripe of mine as I have on numerous occasions had to defend my occupation vociferously to people who thought that I was a gambler. The gambling world has provided me with a very good income for a few years, but in no way am I one of the small percentage of people who use the gambling industry to feed compulsive behavioural disorders... Gripe over, now back to the meeting.

Peter and I met at the bar and then went to sit in the study in front of the log fire with our drinks. Angela and Peter's wife, who I learned was called Jackie, had retired to their respective rooms, leaving Peter and me to talk in comfort about whatever we wanted. After making a fair bit of small talk for the first five or ten minutes, Peter got around to asking me if I was still in gaming.

"Good heavens no, I left the casino industry for good in 1998 and won't ever be going back."

"So what are you doing now then?"

"Well, I'm playing poker professionally and have been for quite some time."

"Oh really, that's very interesting, although it doesn't surprise me given your background."

It never ceases to amaze me how certain people think that just because you've been in one particular avenue of gambling you will have expertise in others. I have even had people ask me for tips on racehorses when I know absolutely nothing about that sport. I told Peter that poker didn't have anything to do with being a croupier. In fact most of the stuff that I've used to train people in how to beat the casinos at blackjack and roulette I've learned after I left the industry.

"Playing poker for a living sounds very glamorous."

"It may be for certain people but not for me. Sitting in front of a computer screen for forty hours a week is far from glamorous."

"No I don't suppose that it is."

"Do you still go in casinos much these days?"

"Too much. Jackie is forever bending my ear about it and saying that I gamble too much."

From what I remember of him, gambling was the last thing that he was doing unless he had been caught. If Peter was telling the truth, and I had no reason to doubt him, not only was he still active but his partner Jackie knew nothing of what he really did otherwise she wouldn't be pestering him like that or maybe she did know but didn't approve and wanted him to stop.

Over the next ten minutes or so, I hit Peter full on with the bombshell that I had known he was cheating back when I was an inspector. I told him about his partnership with Philip and the moves that he was making. I also boosted my ego a little bit by informing him of how I had set him up by enticing him to make moves at certain times that were selected by me. I told him that I knew of his past posting moves on third dozen and also how Philip was using himself as a decoy in order for Peter to make a move.

Peter sat there and said nothing until he finally asked, "Did you say anything to anybody?"

"Do you think that if I did that you would still be going strong today? You were lucky in as much as I was leaving the industry shortly after I detected you, and also that I didn't give a damn about the job."

"Why did you let me cheat on your table, Carl?"

"Like I said, I didn't give a damn and I was immensely interested in what you were doing. I liked your style and I thought at the time that you two were very good and better than anything that I had ever seen in almost ten years."

Peter smiled ruefully and said, "We couldn't have been that good because you spotted us."

I smiled back and laughed and said, "Well, you were going up against one of the best. I estimated that you and Phil were taking about £100 to £200 a night back then. In fact, if you've been active all this time then that must add up to a very tidy sum of money."

"That's not a bad estimate, Carl. I would say that Philip and I have taken on average about £500 a week since you left. I know that we make about twenty-five grand a year and have done for five years."

I whistled and said, "Quarter of a mill and never been barred. That takes some doing today."

"The trick is to keep it small. They don't give a monkeys about a few quid and neither do the punters. Small and often is our motto and we go through night after night and never get noticed by anyone."

"Yeah, but there's more to it than that, Peter. You and Philip had very good acts and your timing was excellent and that's what it is all about."

In my mind, this figure of a quarter of a million pound put them in the category of one of the most successful roulette operations in history. You may say that these figures pale into insignificance compared with past amounts but you have to realise that the amount of knowledge that casino management have now is superior to what they used to have, and so is the equipment and surveillance. Although some of the old moves still have an awful lot of merit simply because many of today's gaming staff simply haven't heard of them.

"Have you ever thought of using what you know to hit the casinos, Carl?"

I shook my head and said "No." At this stage I didn't want the fact that I had been involved with several blackjack teams and that I was responsible for training numerous blackjack players and roulette mechanics to be known by anyone other than the people who were directly involved. Little did I know that I would be writing books about it a few years later. I suppose that if poker hadn't come along these stories would never have been told, as I might have gone back into that business.

But you really have to be careful in this industry because careless talk can cost you an awful lot of money and you really only divulge stuff when it's in your own best interests to do so, or it can't possibly do any harm. As soon as the initial shock of being detected was over and Peter didn't view me as an enemy, quite the opposite, he really started to open up to me.

"You have an excellent memory for faces and events, Carl. You recall stuff that Phil and I were doing years ago as though it was yesterday."

"That's funny. Sometimes I have trouble remembering stuff that I did yesterday, but gambling is a subject that has long since fascinated me and my memory is remarkable for recalling events and data that are connected with it."

Another thing that I didn't mention because it would have created an awkward situation was the fact that I had also suspected Peter's partner Philip of being a pickpocket. I have known a professional pickpocket for a good few years and happen to know a fair bit about the inner workings of that art. Enough to put two and two together when two wallets just happen to go missing from two different punters in the space of a week after they first started entering the casino.

I saw what I thought was a classic two-man move on a poker player who used to turn up on a Wednesday for the tournament and subsequent cash games that we used to have. That very same evening, I overheard this guy speaking to a duty manager asking if any wallets had been handed in. I would have put money on the fact that these two were responsible, though searching them would have been futile as they would have quickly disposed of the evidence, especially in a closed environment like a casino.

I asked Peter if he still worked entirely with Philip. He said he also had another partner further north and they would regularly hit casinos in other areas. The way these guys performed made it look easy, and I suppose it was easy as long as they were doing it.

"When I get home, Carl, would you fancy meeting up and letting me pick your brains? I must confess to feeling a little disturbed about knowing that you knew what we were doing back then. The way I see it, if you spotted us then it's perfectly possible for others to spot us as well and I would like to get some inside info and ideas about how to conceal our moves better. I don't want us to get too complacent and it would be great to talk to someone with your experience and knowledge," remarked Peter.

"Sure, why not. We have an interest in the same thing and I think it will prove illuminating."

We finished our drinks and retired to our rooms. This had proved to be a very interesting conversation and the meeting we had in mind would prove to be equally remarkable.

You Have Already Met, I Take It

The one thing that I love about my job in the gambling industry is the wide variety of people that you get to know and meet. They are highly interesting people from all walks of life, and many of them have done very interesting things and seen exotic places. Not so yours truly, who is so captivated by the gambling industry and beating casinos that he sometimes forgets what life is all about. Surely I could carry on my career in more exotic places, like Las Vegas or Monte Carlo?

But I know that many people would gladly exchange professions with me and this thought helps to keep me on track whenever I start to feel sorry for myself. Although I've met Philip and Peter Montgomery, Rashid Khan, The Salmon and many more, I would have given anything to go back in time and meet people like Joseph Jaggers and William Darnborough, the real pioneers of winning roulette.

Someone once said, "If I have seen further then it is because I have stood on the shoulders of giants." These people were giants and the rest of us have merely followed their lead. But it does make me wonder just how many people are out there right now taking money from the casinos and other gambling establishments by ingenuity and downright chicanery – people who never get detected, and whose activities never get publicised. The figure must run into many millions a year and in today's high-tech age, a much newer type of advantage player is forming.

The Montgomery brothers were not in the same league as some of their more illustrious ancestors, but what they did required skill, and skill that wasn't easily taught. You don't do what they've done for five years without getting caught once without possessing a very considerable amount of skill. In fact, I thought long and hard about putting the contents of these discussions into this book. I did it for two reasons. First, because I wanted the reader to realise that roulette is a highly vulnerable game (as if you needed any more telling); second, because I thought that they would be intrigued to hear what some of these people had to say.

But I would never have mentioned these people if I thought for one second that it would hurt them financially. They know as well as I do that whatever I write about them won't hurt their income as long I don't overstep the mark by identifying them.

The Montgomeries and I had agreed to meet in a pub that was close to where Philip lived. It was a nice homely kind of place as it turned out, with oak beams and a log fire. We soon dispelled with the formalities. Peter just said "You have already met I take it" as his form of introducing me to Philip, and vice versa. Of course, I knew Philip by sight and he knew me, but we had never really spoken to each other during the time we had spent just a few feet apart on different sides of a roulette table.

The meeting wasn't as I had expected. Everything felt informal and relaxed and was just like three regular guys meeting up for a drink to talk about old times. But I knew full well why they wanted to see me: they wanted to increase their knowledge of casino security procedures and to increase their cover.

"Peter tells me that you were on to us from the very beginning."

"Pretty much so, yeah."

Philip smiled and asked, "What makes you so special, then?" in a rather playful way, which wasn't in the least bit aggressive. Mind you, if either of them had shown any aggression towards me, I would simply have walked out and they wouldn't have achieved their objective. At the end of the day, they needed to make friends with someone who knew their operation and not make an enemy of him.

"Carl works as a consultant with casinos regarding cheating and such, and has also been an adviser with a film company on the same thing," said Peter, before I could say any more.

"*Really?*" said Philip in a very surprised tone.

"Yeah, the gaming industry and gaming in general has always held a big fascination with me and I suppose it just kind of started from there really." Getting straight to the point, Philip asked me how I knew about what they were up to from the very start.

"Much of what gave you away to me is rather difficult to explain, but one of the things that gave you away as a potential team was the fact that at no time did you or Peter ever look at each other."

"So, what is so odd about that?" asked Philip.

"Well, if it is taken in isolation then nothing, but when Peter was returning to the table claiming bets, then it's human nature to simply turn your head and look at him, even if only for a few seconds. You never did this, therefore what you were doing or rather not doing was running contrary to human nature, and it was this that told me that something wasn't quite right. Everybody else on the table turned around to look at Peter simply because what had just happened was unexpected to them, and turning around to look to see who was claiming a bet is an instinctive reaction. The fact that you never looked at Peter told me that you must have been either expecting him to do it or that you were deaf. I knew that you weren't deaf so that only left one other explanation in my book."

Philip smiled at Peter and he smiled back, a smile that told me that he knew that I was right.

"So how did you spot our moves when I was obscuring you?"

"Well, first I spotted Peter do a move on another table so I was already on to him."

Philip glanced across at Peter, smiled and said, "Real slick there Pete."

I went on, "As soon as I knew that Peter was a mechanic."

"A what?" interrupted Philip.

"A mechanic is someone who is proficient at cheating; the word first originated on poker with the term card mechanic."

Peter smiled and said, "A polite name for a cheat, Phil!"

I continued, "As soon as I knew that Peter was a mechanic then I not only expected him to do other moves but also to have an accomplice. I knew that if I looked hard enough I would see something else. I just had a funny feeling the moment you walked through the door that you two were together. Hard to put into words. When you came on the same table and went to the top and Pete was at the bottom then I knew that something was coming. Especially when you bought in for purple chips that are very similar to £1 chips. Unknown to you both, I counted the purple colour chips on the table and I knew that they were about half a dozen short, so you had to have passed them to Peter."

"I could have pocketed them."

"Could have, but extremely doubtful especially as I saw you saunter down the table and make some sort of hand contact with Peter. Funny thing was that I used to turn my back on you on purpose just to give you the opportunity to pull the move at exactly the point that I wanted you to."

"What, you mean that you actually manipulated us into doing the move at a certain set time?" exclaimed Philip, to which I simply nodded.

"Bullshit, I don't believe it," exclaimed Philip with a big broad grin on his face.

"Oh, believe it," intervened Peter. "This guy is something else."

May I Suggest An Improvement?

I informed Philip that one of the major factors in their success was their near perfect timing and the fact that they never went for big money. As a team, these two factors were without a doubt their greatest strengths. "From what you've told me so far, you seem to be doing very well without any advice from me," I remarked.

"Yes but we would really appreciate your thoughts, Carl, on

how we could possibly do things better," replied Peter.

"Well in that case may I suggest an improvement?"

"Please by all means do," replied Philip.

"Because you don't go for big money and hit little and often, you really don't have to worry too much about cover as you would if the stakes were higher."

"What do you mean?"

"Well, I really don't see the point with playing in too many casinos; one or two at the most would be best."

"Why? Isn't it better to spread your action around so that no one club can get an angle on you?" remarked Peter.

"Not in this case, no. Remember that you are not card counters or anything like that. Your image is or should be one of just being regular punters. You see, one of the problems that you have when you are a new face is the trust factor. Staff are cautious of people who they don't know in the same way that people are in real life with strangers. It takes time to build up trust, but once staff trust you then your greatest problem has been overcome. You need the staff to begin to view you as part of the furniture and not as a threat. You want them to view you as boring and not worth the effort. Your small action does this to a large extent, but one of the reasons that I spotted you at the outset was because you were new to me. By going to too many casinos then what you are effectively doing is starting from scratch with the trust factor. You must also go out of your way to befriend staff, because no one would suspect that anyone who is really friendly would be robbing their high teeth out."

"I see what you mean," remarked Philip.

I went on, "I'm one of the most difficult people to con simply because I've a very mistrusting nature and am instinctively cynical of human nature. This helps to protect me from any harm most of the time but it does mean that I sometimes mistrust people incorrectly, but I would rather have it this way. What I'm trying to say is that I would still be very vulnerable to being ripped off by people whom I trust. When you trust someone then you don't expect them to con you and this is a tremendous advantage for any con man or thief."

"Isn't that what I was talking about the other week?" remarked Peter. "I've been saying for ages that we need to interact more with the staff but you said that it wasn't a good idea," pointing at Philip. Peter and Philip then got into a little heated debate about the matter, which I was forced to interrupt as it was threatening to get out of hand.

"At the end of the day, you've got away with it, which is a tremendous feat, but your actions can be improved tremendously. It is all about acting the part and bullshitting, and this is what you must strive to do," I said.

"Is there anything else that we could do to improve our play?" asked Philip.

"Yeah, stop nicking wallets." I was gambling with this statement as I had no concrete proof that they had ever taken one, but they were prime suspects for two wallets that went AWOL while I was there. The five to ten seconds of silence before Peter replied told me all I wanted to know.

He laughed in that kind of trying to look cool but really I've just been rumbled kind of a way and said, "What in heaven's name makes you think that we have stolen wallets?"

"Well, two reasons. First, you are stealing money from people on roulette anyway so you are definitely not opposed to theft, are you? Second, because I saw you do it." This was a lie, but I just wanted to have a little bit of fun at their expense and watch them squirm. Without even waiting for a reply or an explanation, I continued. "You were very lucky to get away with that back in '98. One of the punters didn't enquire about his wallet until the following week, when the security tapes had probably been destroyed. I know that there were no cameras in the card room because that's where you took the first one, but the cameras in the pit area could easily have picked something up. You need to give yourself an escape hatch with these kinds of things and pickpocketing is very dangerous inside an enclosed environment."

"Is there anything that you don't fucking spot?" exclaimed Peter.

"Very little, when my mind's on the job," I replied, "but an awful lot when it isn't."

"Well, we stopped doing that routine in 2002 when we had a very close shave inside a casino in Manchester," said Peter.

"It is well within the realm of possibility that you've been clocked somewhere and they are just waiting for another incident before they pull you. They would definitely get the police involved with this sort of thing, because it goes beyond gaming and is a police matter."

"Like we said, we stopped a few years ago," replied Philip.

We carried on the conversation for a further hour or so before I had business elsewhere, but Philip and Peter Montgomery proved to me what an incredible resourceful and intelligent pair they were: £250,000 in the space of five years without ever being detected takes an awful lot of doing… never detected by anyone who cared, that is.

CHAPTER 9

CHEATERS' GALLERY

The contents of this chapter explain techniques that involve actually stealing money. In no way are the publishers or the author recommending or advising anyone to cheat or steal on roulette or any other game for that matter. This chapter merely explains how professional and amateur cheats go about their work and is purely of theoretical interest.

This chapter is really an add-on to the episode with the Montgomeries. Cheating was and still is very prevalent on roulette whether by the house, members of staff or the punters themselves. You've been treated in this book to real accounts from people who cheat for a living and I sincerely hope that you enjoyed that extra touch of realism. But before I go any further let me point out that when I said that casinos cheat, I am referring to backstreet casinos in the vast majority of cases.

Any casino that enjoys more than just a token level of action and imposes strict limits and has sufficient financial backing really doesn't need to stoop to such desperate measures. I've worked in around half a dozen of them for ten years and been in countless others, but I've never experienced cheating on behalf of the house anywhere. The odds that are built into the games defeat the player and all the casino needs to ensure is that the game is being run and played on the level. If it isn't then they could have problems, and that has been the subject of this book.

We have already looked at past posting and chip stealing in the last chapter and will only touch on that again here. But many of the cheating moves that are available on roulette involve the staff and I'll be taking a look at a few of those first. The surveillance in most casinos now is very strict with dealers, inspectors and pit bosses observing the action and managers observing them. Then we have CCTV and even audio detection equipment in some casinos. Another often overlooked method of detection, although not as common, is when a cheat is spotted by other punters and then reported to the management.

Although CCTV can make a casino seem almost impervious to cheating moves, that's a long way from being the truth, especially with many of the cheaper systems. It was relatively easy for me to discover where blind spots were in every casino that I've ever been or worked in. In my last casino before I left the industry, we had a chronic blind spot to the right of AR5 and this was where we were hit three times in the space of three weeks by past posters. I could have informed the management, but I couldn't care less about their money; they were taken to the cleaners by cheats who had about 1 per cent of the skill that the Montgomery brothers had.

If amateurish opportunist cheats can take the casinos for millions every year, what price the professionals? One of their downfalls in my opinion is that they employ the wrong people as security advisers and they pay the price for this. But as I've said earlier in the book, the biggest weakness of any casino is their very own complacency and this is a cheat's greatest weapon.

Once gaming staff get to a certain level of experience, most of them will know numerous ways to cheat the house. Most of them will either not have the inclination or the courage to go down that route, though, and others will fear detection and possible prosecution. Here is a list of ways that money could be extracted from a roulette table by gaming staff, and it is a long way from being exhaustive. I could write an entire book all by itself on ways that croupiers could take money out of casinos.

The Cash Box Move

Situated on every roulette table is a cash box, otherwise known as the drop box. This is a steel box that's locked and situated under the table inside another steel box. It has a slot in the top that coincides with the slot in the table top and it is into this slot that any money goes from punters who have exchanged their cash for chips. The cash gets into the box by way of a plastic plunger, which is not quite as wide as the slot itself and has an opaque handle.

The cash box has a locking mechanism attached to it, which gets reset when the box is emptied during the count (the procedure that's usually done at the end of a shift when all the cash is counted and logged). So to underline what we have here, we have a steel box situated inside another slightly larger steel box with two slots that marry up with each other. But sometimes problems arise with those two slots not being exactly lined up with each other.

It is a common occurrence for cash to lodge in the actual drop box flap after it has been plunged by the dealer. This happens whenever the slots don't line up properly, but it can be manipulated as well. Let us say that a punter has just bought in for £20 worth of chips with a £20 note. What the dealer should do in order to try and make a neat clean drop should be to place the note across the slot in such a way that the slot runs directly across the middle of the note.

Ninety-nine times out a hundred when this is done the note will drop cleanly into the cash box, but sometimes it gets lodged in the cash box lid, underneath the table surface itself and so out of sight of the punters. Not placing the note accurately across the drop box slot increases the frequency of this event happening tremendously. If the dealer knows that they are on the count at the end of the shift, they can plan for this in advance.

The croupiers will be informed at the start of the shift or close to the start if they are on the count or not and can prepare for the move. When the cash box is removed from the steel case that holds it, quite often there will be notes protruding from the slot, which can easily be pulled out by anyone in possession of the box at that time. At the end of the shift, the casino is devoid of punters and most of the staff have left the building, so the number of people who can physically see you has been greatly diminished.

The Fake Call Bet Move

It is a fairly common practice for casinos that take call bets in the middle of the spin to place the bet on the number or numbers to avoid any discrepancy wherever possible. If the call bet has been so late in coming or would take so long to place that it would cause difficulties, it is simply memorised and placed on the wheel. The call bet is declared by the punter and repeated by both dealer and inspector or supervisor.

Throwing call bets across is also an angle that opportunist cheats try to create, especially against inexperienced staff. They hope that they forget the bet, which can be the case if there have been several call bets on the same spin. But just to clear up one small point, there is a difference between verbally declaring a bet from across the room without any money being placed on the roulette table in question and throwing money in the direction of the dealer and making a verbal declaration of the numbers that you want the bet to be placed on, and in what denominations.

In this instance I'm talking about the latter, where money is tossed on the table in front of the dealer and a bet is declared audibly. But this is definitely an avenue where collusion has existed down the years and will continue to do so whenever roulette is dealt in this way and bets like these are allowed. Strangely enough, it doesn't take both the dealer and inspector to be involved in the scam. A rookie trainee dealer is far less likely to remember bets that are thrown their way and especially on a busy game where they'll have numerous other things to think about.

When the bet is placed on the wheel it doesn't take much imagination to realise that if the particular numbers concerned that formed the bet have been forgotten, or maybe the dealer is unsure, then an opportunity for chicanery arises. The rookie dealer will trust the inspector and not even question their word, even if they suspect that they are wrong.

What makes this move very powerful is that it can't be picked up by CCTV. All that any camera would pick up would be the dealer placing the bet on the wheel and the inspector looking on. Only if there was an audible back-up system in place could you detect any wrong doing here... that or being able to lip read.

One of the ways to fool an inexperienced dealer is to make them believe that they have possibly misheard you. This can easily be achieved by a punter stating numbers that sound like another, like seven and eleven for instance, or six and twenty-six. Whenever an inspector is colluding with a punter in this way they tend to wait until they get slow, confused, novice dealers before they try a move like this.

Tripping the Ball

This is another move that can easily be achieved by any inspector who has the nerve to do it. It can also be done by a punter, but the one big draw back to this move is that it is far more likely to be revealed on camera as the move is visual and not audible. It involves subtly and very quickly placing a finger over the rim of the wheel and deflecting the ball from the ball track and into the rotor. Obviously when this is done, care is taken so that the ball is tripped in such a way as to make it go into the desired section that's being bet on.

If you think that this move is very blatant then you would be right, but it is nowhere near as blatant as many people think it is if the timing is right and the cover and diversionary tactics are spot on. The ball is deflected from the ball track when it is coming towards the end of its cycle. This is because it is too noticeable if it is deflected any earlier, as the ball is travelling much too fast for it to drop from the ball track and would look and sound very strange to the dealer and to other punters at the table.

One of the stumbling blocks with this cheating move is that some dealers and many punters tend to look in the wheel while the ball is spinning, and this would make the move impossible. But if you have punters at the table who are busily engaged in placing their bets or doing other things then the possibility of making the move opens up. It is standard practice for the punter who is involved in the scam to distract the dealer at the last possible minute with a call bet. At that exact time, the inspector trips the ball from the ball track into the section that his accomplice is betting on. For good measure, the call bet will be for the same designated area and will provide a very tidy bonus should that bet come in as well.

But in no way is this move confined to being done by an inspector or supervisor. It would be relatively straightforward for any punter to do the same thing, especially in situations where they have very close access to the wheel and the inspectors' attention is split between two tables or there is no inspector present.

For the bet to have a high degree of probability of winning, the bettor places chips on quite a wide area of the wheel, like the tier section. If the wheel is travelling relatively slowly then this increases the profitability and success of the move because a slow-moving wheel means that the target area is hit with a high degree of probability. This is a very daring move, but easy to achieve in the right set of circumstances.

The Payoff Move

This move is as old as the game itself but the casino industry is almost powerless to prevent it on roulette that is dealt by a human dealer. It is the very simple but highly effective process of paying losing bets or bets that were not even there at all. In some cases, bets have been added that were not even there at the beginning of the spin.

The inspector or supervisor doesn't have to be part of this scam. In fact if they were it would complicate the process, because instead of only two people being involved, there would be three. The number of variations that are inherent to this move are absolutely enormous.

The dealer as usual picks and chooses their targets very carefully when it comes to which inspectors to try this against. Some inspectors are extremely lazy or not doing their job properly and are fair game for unscrupulous dealers who are colluding. I must admit that towards the end of my career I was a fair target for this kind of move, simply because I had mentally switched off a large percentage of the time.

The dealers know who the observant inspectors are – they are not always the most experienced ones, either. One of the ways for a dealer to pay a punter off subtly is to deflect chips onto the splits and corners of the winning number while they are clearing the layout or isolating the number. This can be done very well by even a moderately skilled dealer; even if the move was observed by another punter, it would just look for all the world like a careless and sloppy dealer.

Any bet that's on a split gets paid to the sum of 17 to 1 and 8 to 1 for a corner bet and those odds are not small change. The number of times that I've accidentally removed chips from around the winning number from splits and corners when I've been isolating the number is too numerous to mention. It would have been just as easy for me to slide a losing chip onto a winning split or corner as well, and I've accidentally done this many times.

Another way to pay off a punter is to slide a losing chip from the layout onto one of the dozens of columns. Once again this move is highly dependent on the inspector being relatively unobservant, which many are. As far as many of the casinos in England go, many inspectors deem that they are not paid enough and most of the action is just too repetitive for them to remain focused throughout the entire shift.

As the Montgomery brothers knew, the secret to this is not to get too greedy. Inspectors will mentally tighten up if substantial cash chip action starts to hit the felt. In fact, even the placing of one single chip that's of a higher denomination to anything else that's on the table will get mentally logged.

The Blocker

The blocker move is really just another variation on past posting, but instead of the move being made on a number, the target for attack is the high numbers. To explain, for the benefit of anyone who isn't overly familiar with roulette, the game has thirty-six numbers and zero. There are all types of bets available, of which one is to be able to bet on either low or high numbers. Low numbers are those from 1 to 18 and the high numbers are 19 to 36. To bet on low or high numbers, you don't have to physically place a chip on all of the numbers from 1 to 18 or 9 to 36. Placing your bet on the box designated 1 to 18 or 19 to 36 will do the same job.

But the betting square for high numbers is at the bottom far corner of the table, which is the furthest away from the inspector. This opens up a potential move and the three-man blocker move exploits this to the full. The timing is everything with this move, as it is with most moves. As the ball is falling into the number, the dealer signals whether the ball is in a low or high number. The signal is pre-arranged and only known to the dealer and their accomplices.

At that precise moment, one of the team leans across the table to straighten a bet or place a late bet. This is done in a seemingly harmless way; the move isn't only a diversion, but it also forms a barrier between the inspector and the bottom of the table, especially the outside bet section. The third member of the team then places a sure-fire-winning bet on the high numbers and gets paid even money.

As long as the bet is for a relatively small amount of money nothing gets noticed, and because the past posting has been done on high numbers and not on a straight-up number it never seems to get detected. It amazes me how many so-called experienced gaming staff only ever look out for past posting on the numbers. This blinkered vision makes them fair game for moves like the blocker.

The move is even more effective whenever somebody else is betting on high numbers, because their bet can assist the cheater at the bottom of the table in being able to conceal the bet on high numbers behind somebody else's bet. In fact it is common with this type of move for the guy in the middle who late bets also to place a bet on high numbers himself, in order for the higher denomination chip to be concealed. Let me explain.

One of the team members buys in for a fair-sized amount of colour and places sporadic bets on the layout, but he also places an entire stack of colour chips on high numbers. A stack of 25p colour chips will dwarf a single higher denomination chip and easily conceal it. The stack of chips will only amount to £5 and this bet will be close to breaking even, anyway, in the long run, but the £25 chip that's a certain winner on high numbers will more than compensate for that. This is the sheer power of the blocker move.

The Concealed Push Out Move

As I've said many times, the key to taking money from roulette is to keep it small and to make it look natural. You may get away with winning or taking large amounts of money for a short while because the casino can't be sure that you are not just getting lucky and will be reticent to intervene. It is far more productive in the long run to go for small and regular amounts, because when taken over time these will add up to more money, unless we are talking about a very substantial one-off coup.

The concealed push out move has been another very common cheating technique over the years and once again involves the dealer. The move is relatively simple: a punter buys in for four or more stacks of colour chips that resemble the colour of the cash chip that's about to be concealed. The reason for the colour similarity is because the dealer needs the move to appear natural if they get detected.

A much higher denomination chip is mixed in with a stack of colour chips. The stack with the cash chip in it will be situated behind two more stacks of colour as you push them out to the punter. Also, your guiding hand will conceal the chip to anyone else on the table as well, thus making it truly invisible.

To strengthen the move, the dealer plans for it in advance. If someone has been playing in black £25 chips this provides an ideal opportunity to create the move without it looking suspicious if you get caught. As the £25 chips are scooped into the chipping machine with all of the other chips, they should in theory be separated into their respective colours by the machine.

But cash chips often come through the machine and go into one of the chutes that has colour chips in it, thus making what is called a "dirty stack". As the dealer is compiling the five stacks of colour in order to pass them out to their accomplice who has just bought in, they casually remove a stack of colour chips from the machine with the "dirty chip" in it or, in this case, a £25 chip. If the machine has kept the cash chips separate, it wouldn't be too difficult for any dealer to do this manually while the inspector is busy watching the other table. This is something that they will almost certainly be doing if the ball is dropping on that table and especially if that dealer is a trainee.

So the cheating dealer has ample time to construct a dirty stack of their own in order to pass it out to their accomplice, who in turn pockets the £25 and is literally playing for free with the £25 of colour. With an unobservant inspector, this trick can be repeated many times and as long as the player is careful with the cashing-out process they are very unlikely to get detected.

The Colour Mark Up Move

Not all roulette tables offer the same denomination colour chips simply because not all tables are playing to the same stakes. There can be 25p tables, 50p tables, £1 tables, £5 tables etc. This means that each colour chip on the respective table is of that denomination. But you don't have to go onto a 50p table to be able to play with 50p chips. In many casinos, punters can go onto a 25p table and ask to be marked up at 50p. The dealer will notify the inspector about their request and a 50p marker is used to signify that the colour chips that are being used by that particular punter are to a value of 50p per chip and not 25p.

Playing with colour chips that are higher than all of the other chips on the table creates many possible moves for a rogue dealer or inspector for that matter. Once again, a serious opportunity arises for a cheating dealer whenever the inspector is preoccupied on the other table.

It would be the easiest thing in the world for a punter to pass a dealer £30, for example, and the dealer to pass the player six stacks of colour instead of three. If the move is detected by the inspector, the dealer just acts as if he thought that the colour was in 25p chips and temporarily forgot. It is very difficult to prove that a dealer is deliberately intending to cheat in this way. The reason for the oversight could be that the dealer is tired or distracted for some reason. Even if an inspector suspected that something was amiss, it is still very difficult to prove any intent on behalf of the dealer.

Inspectors trust experienced dealers not to make mistakes and supervise them to the absolute minimum, especially if there is a big game or a relative trainee dealer on the other table. The inspector generally looks for the other dealer clearing the wrong number and that's about it. In certain casinos the procedures can be a lot stricter and many casinos don't allow the inspector to interfere with a dealer's game at all.

All savvy dealers know which inspectors are observant and which are not, and also when the times arise when an inspector is distracted or upset. It is quite possible that a dealer could be passing money to a punter without incurring any personal gain themselves. Many dealers do this for a multitude of reasons. Some do it because they feel sorry for the punter because they are persistently losing heavily or because they like them as people. Others do it for reasons of sexual interest or physical attraction. But these gratuitous payouts go on all the time and they are costing the casino industry millions of pounds a year in this country and heaven only knows how much worldwide.

The Chipping Machine Scam

There is no real name for what I'm about to tell you so I've dubbed this move "the chipping machine scam" for want of a better title. The reason that I include this scam is because it once happened inside a casino where I worked and a dealer and an inspector were both found to be involved in the operation. As had already been stated, many roulette tables have chipping machines to assist with the heavy action that games sometimes get.

The chips are cleared from the layout after the spin is completed and scooped into a black plastic funnel down into the machine. There is an electronic eye inside the machine, which can identify different colours. The chips are sorted inside the machine and come up through chutes, which are just a fraction wider than the chips themselves. Only chips of a certain colour will come up one chute and the dealer then takes them out of the machine in stacks of twenties.

In several of the casinos where I worked, it was standard procedure to keep the cash chips from going down the chute after the spin if they were higher than a certain denomination, but this couldn't always be avoided because of the heavy action that you sometimes get, especially with games only being at either 25p per chip or 50p per chip.

But sometimes cash chips and colour chips would fall through tiny gaps in the plastic chute or elsewhere and end up inside the machine itself. Sometimes this gets noticed and sometimes it doesn't. What tends to happen is that several cash chips are taken out of circulation because they fall into the machine. At the end of the shift, it was standard practice where I worked for the inspector present at the table at the end of the shift to take the back off the chipping machine and check it for chips that had fallen inside, whether cash chips or colour chips.

This involved bending down below waist height so you were out of sight of anyone else. It was the easiest thing in the world for a dealer or inspector to take the cash chips and hide them on their person. Usually the best place would be down a sock or shoe, but there are numerous places where a croupier could hide a single chip and it not be detected. This is why croupiers and inspectors can't wear shirts or trousers with pockets in them in many casinos.

The pair of cheats where I worked would subtly hide the cash chips on their person. Then they got a punter who was known to them to cash the chips in for them as they obviously couldn't do this themselves. But one of the flaws in this scam is that the casino does what is called a chip count at the end of every shift, so they know how many chips are missing from the casino and in what denomination. They also know on what dates these chips go missing and on what dates they come back.

The longer this goes on, a pattern is slowly formed and it would be easy for any casino to check back on the staff rotas and find out who was working on the shifts that the chips went missing. The more times that chips go missing the easier it is to find out who the culprit is when you check back in this way. But these two croupiers were far from being the only casino employees to benefit from the chipping machine scam.

The Wooden Horse

In ancient Greek mythology, there was a tale of a group of soldiers who hid inside the framework of a wooden horse in order to get access to a city that had been under siege. I'm sure that you have heard of the story. This story takes us into our next move in our cheaters' gallery, the wooden horse move.

This scam is another of those moves that's almost as old as the game itself and it surprises me that it still has any life left in it at all, after all its publicity down the years. A punter can perform this move all by himself and doesn't need an accomplice or any help from the dealer or inspector.

As the ball is about to fall into the number, the cheat places a bundle of money onto high numbers. The reason why he places the bet on high numbers is twofold. First, the dealer has further to stretch to pick the money up. Second, the bet on high numbers is on a portion of the layout that's situated directly in front of the cheater and this gives him the opportunity to pick the bet back up. The cheat places a bundle of money on high numbers with the lowest denomination note on the outside and higher denomination notes concealed on the inside.

He does this at the last possible second before the ball drops so the dealer doesn't have the time to place the bet with cash chips and will just merely call "cash plays high numbers to the maximum". Although I said that this move can be done alone, having an accomplice increases the profitability of the move. If the ball drops into a low number the cheat takes the money back off the layout at the precise split second that he knows that the bet is lost. The inspector will see this and demand to the punter that he puts this money back. Of course, unknown to the dealer and inspector, the cheat has switched the bundles and places what appears to be the same bundle back on high numbers with a profound apology as drawing attention to himself – upsetting the staff is not very high on his list of priorities. Inside the other bundle are notes of either the same denomination or lower as the notes on the outside, depending on whether the bet has won or lost.

It is blatantly obvious to anyone what the advantage is here. If the bet wins, which it will do almost 50 per cent of the time, then the bet is simply left on. But if the bet loses it is switched for the other bundle that has substantially less money in it. If a cheater could get away with this scam just once a night they could earn a very serious amount of money by the end of the year.

CHAPTER 10

THE MIRAGE ON THE TABLE

Another name for this book could have been "The Good the Bad and the Ugly of Roulette". We have seen the good by way of some of the absolutely ingenious methods that certain individuals have used in order to beat the game. We have also looked at the bad, in the form of the plethora of cheating moves and downright skulduggery that casinos have had to contend with down the years. What we have not seen yet is the downright ugly, and that is the purpose of this chapter. So ugly in fact that what you are about to read is not even a way to beat the game at all. What I'm talking about is the large number of systems that punters use of varying complexities to try and get an advantage over the game. Some of these systems are so ingeniously compiled and so vociferously touted by their exponents that there is really only one thing wrong with them… they don't work!

With the invention of the internet came an army of charlatans and con men using the information superhighway as a tool to trap the desperate, the naïve and the gullible. Most of the avenues have been used by the con man and roulette is no different. I've seen numerous adverts and websites by some guy claiming this and that about roulette and asking for money at the end. Many of these "systems" are in fact *systems* themselves. Let me make one thing absolutely clear to you right here and now:

There is no mathematical system known to man
that can overcome the house edge on roulette!

Trust me, if there was then I would certainly know about it and so would the gaming industry after all this time. Some of the greatest mathematicians on the planet over the past several hundred years have tried and failed but yet some guy on a website has the answer. There are ways to beat roulette, countless ways in fact, and this book has touched on many of them but systems are not one of them.

If you are presently using a system in the belief that it will earn you money then stop now before it gets too late. If you've paid for a system then you've been ripped off plain and simple and don't hold your breath when it comes to getting your money back. In fact, I'm going to repeat the line above just for good measure.

There is no mathematical system known to man
that can overcome the house edge on roulette!

There, I've repeated it just in case you overlooked it the first time. If you still persist in using a "system" after reading that then I'm sorry but your naivety deserves what it gets. Just so that you are fully aware of what I mean by systems, I'll go into detail about some of the more common betting systems that have been in use down the years and, sadly, still are. I feel that the title of this chapter is very apt because "mirages" are exactly what they are.

The Martingale

The Martingale system is by far the most popular and universally used betting system on roulette and comes top of the mirage list. Like most systems on roulette, the Martingale is what is known as a doubling-up system or "progression" system.

This system is as old as roulette itself and dates back to the 17th century. The doubling of the stakes is performed on the even chance bets, be it high or low numbers, black or red or odd or even. The basic method of the system would be something like putting £1 on red and if it lost then placing £2 on red on the next spin. If that lost then place £4 on the next spin, then £8, £16 and so on.

At first glance, this seems to be a foolproof way to make money as Mr Naïve can't see anyway that black can keep coming up that amount of times. He tries to be smart about it and looks for situations where there have been three blacks on the trot before he starts to bet red. In his mind, red is behind to the tune of three bets and so is due. He also thinks that doing something like this will prevent him from reaching the table maximum.

His confidence is high after a long succession of small wins and he can't imagine that disaster could be just around the corner. But it is the succession of small wins of £1 that fuel the delusion that this system is an easy money maker. I've seen countless system players down the years and have witnessed numerous players start to sweat as they are nearing the maximum. But that's precisely why the maximums are there in the first place, to prevent the casino from being vulnerable to system players slowly bleeding money out of them.

There are a number of variations attached to the Martingale but each variation does absolutely nothing to change the house advantage. There is the "reverse Martingale" in which the player doesn't retrieve their bet after it wins but leaves it on. There is also a variation of the Martingale, where the player doubles their bet and adds one extra chip after a loss. Once again, we have the same result... inability to overcome the house edge.

In many casinos, the table limits are around two hundred times what the minimum bet is on even chances. So if the minimum on even chances is £10 then the maximum is £2,000 and so on. At several of the casinos where I worked the maximums were even more restrictive on system players on certain tables. There was one table that had a £5 minimum on even chances with a £500 maximum, a ratio of only 100 to 1.

One of the main reasons why the Martingale and other systems of a similar nature are still with is today is because people still win with them. It is perfectly possible when using these systems that a big loss could be an awful long time in coming when you need a relatively lengthy series of numbers to go against you. Also, depending on how often you play roulette it could take years for that big wipe-out to arrive, if it ever does. But any conventional betting system on roulette has a negative expectation and that can't change.

If a national lottery player scooped the jackpot and won several million pound, if they continued to do the lottery until they died, they would still be a very substantial amount of money ahead during the course of their lifetime. It is exactly the same principle with system players. Casinos loathe them but not because they are a threat to their bottom line. They dislike them because the minute that they see them walk through the door they know that they are likely going to be walking out again not having lost any money. What tends to happen with the ones that do get wiped out is that the big loss puts them off ever playing again, so the casino doesn't get any more money out of them after they realise that the system that they thought was working is in fact seriously flawed.

Even on a table with a one hundred to two hundred spread on even chances, after eight consecutive losing bets the next bet takes you over the maximum. So eight consecutive losers and nine at the most wipes you out completely. I've lost count of the number of times that I've witnessed a run of nine spins on the trot on a particular even chance bet. The most I ever witnessed in almost ten years was twenty-two consecutive reds... Still think that you are safe now?

The Labouchere

I sometimes think that the fancy-sounding names of some of these systems contribute to an awful lot of people using them. If they had boring, unimaginative names I certainly don't think they would be as popular as they are. The Labouchere is a system that in many ways is a lot better than the Martingale, simply because the maximums are more difficult to reach and a player is highly unlikely to get their entire bankroll wiped out.

This system is based on cancelling numbers out and betting as a result. I'm not going to go into the details of the Labouchere system and waste time and space here by telling you how to do it, simply because I don't want you or anyone else for that matter using the damn things. Don't get me wrong here, if you were to have a one-off visit to a casino then using a system like the Labouchere would give you a very high probability of coming out of the building winning money. The problem is that people don't know when to quit with these things and play them out until it blows up in their face. The Labouchere also has a twin brother called the "reverse Labouchere", which came to fame in the now famous book *Thirteen against the Bank* as mentioned earlier in the book. Anyone reading or hearing about that book would be forgiven for thinking that systems are the way to go and that casinos can't defend against them.

This is rubbish. The casinos involved in that highly entertaining book put a halt to their action. They had lost a very considerable sum of money to Leigh's team and were unaware of exactly what they were doing. Also Leigh and his band of merry men and women only played the system for about two weeks at the most. This is a very short length of time in the life of any mathematical system and it is a cast iron certainty that if the casinos had allowed them to continue then they would have lost everything that they had won, plus their bankroll.

Another factor with the "reverse Labouchere" is that the bankroll needs to be much higher than many of the other systems, making it a very expensive system to operate and beyond the capability of many players. This was why in Leigh's book, it stated that the twelve members of the team had each put a share of the bankroll up to spread the financial burden. But it surprises me that even now in the 21st century many small-time casinos will not tolerate system players. Changing the subject for a brief moment to blackjack, there used to be a system player who played that game while I was still working in the industry. He would play basic strategy coupled with a progressive betting system that was difficult to beat most of the time. At times it seemed that he would turn up and leisurely walk away with £300–400.

This punter who was called Thomas was a very distinguished gentleman and a joy to deal to. But when he lost, he went for a very big score indeed, because he was escalating his bets in a very similar way, only this time it was on blackjack instead of roulette. When people play like this they can escape the hangman's noose for an awful long time. But after I left the industry, I discovered that one of the casinos where I worked barred the guy from playing there all because it was "messing up their figures", as one gaming manager informed me one evening.

A move to bar a person like this isn't based on sound mathematical principles but highlights how casinos loathe system players, though not because they threaten them. It is simply because they know that the return that they will get from these punters will be lower than from other more reckless punters and the big wipe-out could be an awful long time in coming. This is why players get seduced by systems, because the illusion of easy money is a very powerful one indeed.

There's an almost infinite number of systems, but many are simply variations of the same system. In fact it would be more correct to say that there are an almost infinite number of "variations" to systems. The rather attractive-sounding D'Alembert and its cousin the "reverse D'Alembert" are two more very popular systems that have stood the test of time. Some users of the more modified and technical systems have gone a long time in between losses or never encountered losses at all over very long periods of time.

This has led to a widespread opinion in certain circles that it is possible to beat roulette by using a mathematical system. I for one don't rule out anything and wouldn't totally rule out systems being able to beat the game. To say that something is impossible is a committal statement. Just because we have failed to find an answer to something over the space of about two hundred and fifty years doesn't mean that something is impossible.

But I've yet to see proof that systems provide a long term positive expectation so I can only base my opinion on what I know at this time and this is that it isn't possible to beat the game by these methods based on what we know today. But who knows what we will know tomorrow or next year. I mean if a system player was successful over the space of three years then this would hardly prove that his particular system was working.

Many professional poker players can and have run both good and bad for very long periods of time. As I said earlier with the national lottery example, if you had no prior knowledge of the fact that the expectation of doing the lottery was in the negative and you were lucky enough to win straight away, then it would take you dozens upon dozens of lifetimes to prove that you couldn't make money by playing the national lottery.

I know one thing is certain, though. If the holy grail of the perfect mathematical system is out there waiting to found, I know of one person who will not be wasting their time in order to try and find it.

CHAPTER 11

FACT OR FICTION?

I leave you to decide whether the content of this chapter is fact or fiction, but what you are about to read is based on events that all happened to a certain extent. The names are fictitious and so is the name of the chemical substance that's used, but this chapter tells the story of what could easily be a real scam perpetrated against a casino. It once again underlines how vulnerable casinos are, especially when you include inside assists. Like I said, the characters in this chapter are fictitious, but the events are certainly not based on fantasy.

The year was 1991 and Duncan Elway and Matthew Mcdermott were having a meeting at Matthew's house to discuss the possibility of hitting a casino from the inside. Like many other people, they were seduced by the thought of scams and were enthralled by the tales of con men and swindlers. There has always been something appealing and loveable about some of these characters and that's partly why they interest people so much. There is an element of the crook in all of us, because of how exciting the life sometimes seems from the outside, but Matthew and Duncan have taken this interest to another level and situated inside Matthew's basement is a full-sized roulette wheel made by the Paul Tramble roulette wheel company in Reno. The wheel appears to be in excellent condition and the metallic rotor, canoes, frets and spindle still glimmer and shine like new under the single light that illuminates Matthew's basement.

Where Matthew came by the wheel he is certainly not prepared to say, but roulette wheels like these can be bought on the open market these days and reconditioned ones can be purchased for a couple of grand. Matthew had his own double glazing business, which was hardly pulling any trees up by way of profit and it would be no surprise if the entire thing folded. Matthew was certainly not averse to folding businesses as he had done so several times before and had been officially declared bankrupt. He owed his business associates considerable sums of money, but that didn't bother Matthew and he never lost any sleep over.

Duncan worked on reception at the casino near to where Matthew lived and he and Matthew had been very good friends for a long time, since they were school kids in fact. Because of their close friendship, Duncan would regularly reveal information to Matthew that ordinary punters wouldn't have had access to. Duncan was very close friends with an assistant general manager who worked there, close enough to find things out that would interest a charlatan like Matthew.

Matthew would know first hand how the casino had done on any particular shift, if they had met their targets, who was being promoted and all kinds of confidential stuff. Duncan was a likeable guy and even the gaming staff would open up to him and tell him information simply because everyone trusted him. Nobody perceived him as a threat and he appeared to love his job as he was always smiling and telling jokes.

But this just served to mask his true feelings. In fact he was very disgruntled with his job and resentful that he hadn't had a pay rise in a long time. He hated the fact that some punters were very rude to him but being good friends with the assistant general manager put him into a very awkward situation, because he had got Duncan the job in the first place so to complain now would seem like ingratitude. Duncan always knew just how dodgy Matthew was, but the two of them had a lot more in common than being life-long friends and good drinking buddies. They shared a very unhealthy interest in scams and con men and would sometimes talk for hours devising intricate theoretical cons either at Duncan's place or round at Matthew's.

As both of them were single this was easy. Duncan was recently divorced and Matthew was doing what he had always done and that was to flit from partner to partner never staying with any girl more than a few months. Over the years they had discussed ways to rip off banks, credit card companies, motorists, just about anybody and anything. But because of Duncan's job, Matthew had never before brought up the subject of ripping off a casino… until tonight.

It was the very first time that Matthew had revealed to Duncan that he had a full-sized proper roulette wheel, which had seen action inside a real casino. Duncan was amazed by this and asked how long he had had it. When he found out that Matthew had owned it for over three years, Duncan was very surprised.

"Why didn't you tell me about the wheel before, can't you trust me or something?"

"It's not that, I just didn't want to put you into an awkward position, but with you looking for another job and having that interview on Thursday I figured that you won't be in the industry for much longer."

Duncan smiled and said "What's the matter? Did you think that I would blab?"

"No, not at all, it just didn't feel right, that's all."

"So what have you been doing with it and have you found a way to beat the thing?"

"Maybe," replied Matthew, with a distinct twinkle in his eye.

"Come on then, tell your good buddy."

"At first I tried to spin certain numbers, but I couldn't do it and after about six months I packed it in. Then I tried to do the opposite and spin away from certain sections and I thought that I was succeeding at this at first, but that proved to be a red herring as well. Over the past three years I've tried all kinds of things to beat this damn wheel, but the task has proved to be very difficult."

"But you've found a way, haven't you?"

"In theory. I've yet to try it out and won't be able to until next week."

"So, come on then, what is it?"

"Well, I stumbled on the idea really while playing tennis and it's quite simple. You know that if you threw a tennis ball at numerous different surfaces then the degree of bounce on that ball would relate to how hard each surface was?"

"That and how hard you threw it."

"I know that, but let's suppose that we could throw it evenly and at the same speed each time, then the bounce would be identical for each surface, would it not?" Duncan nodded in silent agreement. "Well the ball on a roulette wheel falls from the track as soon as its speed falls to a certain point, and that speed is constant from spin to spin. So because the metal rotor is made of the same material, the bounce will be the same in the wheel."

"Yeah, but you still can't predict where the ball is going to bounce to."

"Yes, but I read about a case some while ago where someone got access to a roulette wheel after the casino was closed and inserted black rubber strips into the number slots that were identical in size. The following day when the casino opened they went back and started betting heavily on red, because the ball would simply not come to rest in any of the black numbers that had the much springier rubber strips in them."

"That's brilliant."

"Yeah it is, but it's also impractical."

"What do you mean?" replied Duncan with a puzzled look on his face.

"Well, for a start, I just can't see how the black rubber strips are going to be the same shade of black as the natural black that's in the wheel. Those strips would stand out a mile."

"Couldn't you put a black rubber strip into every black number in the wheel so that there wouldn't be a colour difference?"

"You could, but that has two very distinct problems. First, having a rubber strip in every single black number would mean that red numbers would hardly ever come out because the ball would naturally seek out the least line of resistance. Second, placing rubber strips in the wheel is just providing the casino with evidence for which they can prosecute someone. No, what's needed is a way to get the exact same effect without leaving any evidence at all and it being a lot more invisible than placing rubber pads into the number slots."

"So what do you propose?"

"Well, I had this idea to smear an opaque resin-type substance on the black numbers that would be invisible to the naked eye. When the ball hit the number pocket it wouldn't be making contact with the metal but the resin substance instead, which would have a far different level of bounce than the ordinary metal pockets."

"Does this substance exist?"

"You bet your life it does. I know this guy who is a lab technician for a chemical company and he says that Oxydysetomide would do what I was looking for. The stuff can be applied and sets like varnish in a few seconds. But the best thing about it is that the substance can be removed by applying petrol afterwards and this breaks it down enough for it to be removed."

"What's it called again?"

"Oxydysetomide."

"But you still have the problem of too many reds coming up and the casino getting suspicious very quickly."

"That's simple enough to get around. All you do is smear half of the black numbers and leave the other half. That way, it will just look as though there is a surplus of red numbers happening. In fact, even if the ratio of reds to blacks was as high as two to one for an entire shift, I really don't think that they would notice. I'm meeting this guy called Ian next week and he's giving me a bottle of the stuff. I'm going to try it on my wheel to see what happens. I also want to see how long it takes to get the stuff back off again. My wheel is a few years old but it will do the job for what I want."

"Can you trust this guy?"

"I've not told him what I want it for and he hasn't asked."

"But what if it works, then what? I mean you surely aren't just doing this for theoretical reasons, Matt, are you?"

"Maybe, maybe not."

"Why don't you just say it?"

"Say what?" asked Matthew, with an I-don't-know-what-you're-talking-about look on his face.

"You know exactly what I'm talking about. If you're not thinking about it now then the thought will cross your mind eventually. You're just too devious not to have thought of it. You know full well that I have access to the casino after hours and that I'm the only person in the entire building until about seven or eight in the morning," remarked Duncan. Without even bothering to reply to Duncan's question, Matthew forged ahead by revealing his plan.

"The way that I see it, we only have two potential problems that could be difficult to get around, and the first one is the cameras," remarked Matthew.

"The cameras could be got around very easily," interrupted Duncan "but what is the other problem?"

"The problem with the wheel covers and the plastic seals that they use that are individually numbered. They would know that the cover had been removed and put back."

"I don't think that it would be a problem here. I've watched the afternoon staff remove the covers and just throw the seals in the bin. Nobody checks them, they just don't seem to give a fuck. Nothing happens here from week to week and they just go through the day on autopilot most of them. I could easily get my hands on a couple of seals and the ones that were taken off could easily be replaced. If they can't be bothered to check them then they wouldn't notice that the serial numbers were different," responded Duncan enthusiastically.

"Yeah, and even if someone did notice then would they really think that something was seriously amiss anyway? I mean they would just think that someone had written down the wrong numbers on the pit sheet," added Matthew excitedly.

"What's your plan for the cameras then, Duncan?"

"Simple. I could easily get access to the key for the office door. All I have to do is get a spare key cut and – bingo! We have our very own office door key. Inside the office are the controls to the cameras, what they are viewing and from what angle. I know how they operate and I can fix it so one of the roulette wheels is out of view for a short period. How long would it take to take the cover off, apply the stuff and put the cover back on and reseal it?"

"Five minutes tops, but you would have to let me in."

"That would be a problem because the car park camera would pick you up and so would the camera on reception."

"Hmm, that's a problem."

They sank into silence for a few seconds until Matthew burst out: "Got it!"

"What?"

"I don't have to enter the building at all because you are already there. You are already beyond the car park camera and you've worked there for so long that you're almost above suspicion. I would imagine that the application process could be done by anybody and all you would have to do would be to go back in there and remove the evidence after we had hit them."

Duncan grinned and asked, "So I'm the one doing the dirty work am I?"

"It's just the easiest solution, that's all."

"Let me get one thing absolutely straight. Are you saying that this thing is a goer? I mean that you are prepared to do this thing where I work?" asked Duncan in a very surprised tone, verging almost on shock.

"Because you would be the one who was taking the risk, you would get 50 per cent of whatever we won. I think that this is fair because I'm putting the money up and would be placing the action and also getting and paying for the Oxydycetamide, so I would want half also," replied Matthew.

"All this stuff didn't just come to you tonight, Matt, did it? You must have already thought this shit up before you came here."

"I have to confess that this is true, but until I road test the Oxy then it isn't a definite goer yet."

"But what if the results prove positive?"

"Then we'll talk about things, but not a word to anyone, Duncan, about this."

"Do you really need to say that to me after all we've been through down the years?"

"I know, but I'm just paranoid. Anyway, let's wait and see shall we?" replied Matthew. With that they parted company and went their separate ways. All great in theory but theory has a nasty habit of blowing up in your face. Mainly because something gets overlooked or because something unexpected happens and everything gets messed up. But this seemed safe as Duncan would be the only person in the entire building for several hours and he had total access to the cameras and the wheels.

Matthew's real problem was getting Duncan to agree to it, because it would be very difficult otherwise for him to pull this off successfully and he knew this only too well. Matthew and Duncan had been friends for a long time and he didn't want this to come between them. He knew that Duncan was far from happy in his job, but undertaking to do something like this is really something else again. Time will tell us many things and the real test with the Oxydycetamide was only a few days away.

The Acid Test

Matthew had met Ian at lunch time on Monday in a local café near where Ian worked. It was Ian's lunch hour but this was more than enough time for them to meet and exchange the substance. All Ian wanted for the Oxy was a hundred quid, which was easy pocket money to him as he could get the stuff in whatever quantity you wanted and it had no real value by itself.

Apparently the Oxy was a derivative of several other substances combined. It had a transparent look like water, except when you tilted the glass beaker, it was a lot thicker. Ian had informed Matthew that the Oxy had a smell but that it would wear off after several hours. This could cause another potential problem and one that Matthew had not foreseen. The Oxy would begin to solidify after about a minute so Duncan couldn't hang around in applying the stuff and he certainly had to be careful getting it onto his fingers and hands. Matthew and Ian soon parted company and Matthew literally couldn't wait to get home and try the Oxy on his own wheel.

As soon as he arrived home, he fixed himself a cup of coffee and went downstairs into his basement and took the plastic polythene sheet from his wheel. He had a small red brush for applying the Oxy as it was thin enough to be applied with a brush according to Ian. Within a few minutes, Matthew had applied the Oxy to nine of the eighteen black numbers in his wheel. In fact he had done the last number before the first had fully set. Ian was not wrong about this stuff having a strong smell, Matthew thought. He was getting quite high being in such close proximity to the stuff.

There, that was it, half of the black numbers had been coated with the Oxy and Matthew stood back to look at his handywork. He couldn't believe what he was seeing, the stuff was invisible except for a faint difference in shine between the numbers that were coated and the numbers that were not. Matthew set to work spinning the ball and recording the numbers almost at once, and by the end of the evening had recorded 500 spins. The results were nothing short of remarkable: out of those 500 spins no fewer than 359 of them were black, which amounted to black numbers coming in at a whopping 72 per cent of the time.

Matthew did a few quick calculations on some scrap paper and found that out of an average sample of 500 spins that red and black would come up on average about 48 per cent of the time each when rounded up or down with the single zero accounting for the difference. But the Oxy had increased these odds dramatically. What appeared to be happening was that the numbered slots that included the resin were exhibiting considerably less bounce than the other normal number slots and the ball was simply finding the least line of resistance. Suddenly the thought entered Matthew's head that he could have had a far greater return if he had been betting on the black numbers that had the resin in them. But would this only serve to alarm the casino staff and management too early?

What you couldn't do with any gambling scam was to be too greedy. It is greed plain and simple that gets people caught. The discipline would be that this would be a one hit affair and one hit only. After the petrol had removed the Oxy then all evidence would have been removed and the casino staff would be none the wiser, though this would involve Duncan going back in a second time and this would involve further risk.

Still, Matthew wasn't convinced about this sample size of 500 spins being accurate and he decided to do a second sample the following day. He spent all the following morning spinning the ball and writing down the numbers and the black numbers arrived at a rate of 66 per cent for the second batch. Still wanting further clarification, after lunch he embarked on a third batch of

500 spins, which when completed showed black coming up 71 per cent of the time. This was it as far as Matthew was concerned, the Oxy worked, but he still didn't like the difference in shine between the number slots that had the resin in them from the slots that didn't.

Then an idea struck him: what if he tried the Oxy inside a red pocket? Maybe, just maybe, there would be a difference, but it sure wouldn't hurt to try. He applied the Oxydycetamide to number 3, which is a red number, and waited for it to set. The result was amazing. This time he couldn't see any difference whatsoever in the shine as the red colour seemed to be taking it better. Just to be doubly sure, he would do another set of results only this time on the red numbers and see what happened, although there was no obvious reason for it not to work on the red numbers.

But that would have to wait for another day as he was starting to get a little fed up with being in his basement all day and not having seen daylight. Matthew placed the plastic dust sheet over the wheel and went back upstairs. Seeing the Oxy or rather not seeing it in the red number made him feel very excited. He fixed himself some supper as he realised that he had barely eaten anything since lunch. No sooner had he eaten this than he retired to bed to dream about his big hit on the casino.

This was where the doubts and the demons started to appear. Question after question ran through his head. Would Duncan agree to do it or would he bottle it? Would the Oxy have the same effect on the casino wheels as it had on his because of possible differences in the metal? Would it look invisible on the casino wheel? On and on it went until Matthew finally fell asleep some time after two in the morning. Tomorrow would be another day.

The Second Run

At least one thing could be certain and that was that the smell of the Oxy resin wore off after a couple of hours, which was easily long enough. Matthew had proved that yesterday during its opening trial. Having awoken at just after eight, he realised that any further sleep was futile and decided to get up. He had a business to run, but what the hell, he had staff who could manage in his absence.

He went down into his basement and applied the Oxy to exactly half of the red numbers in the same way as he had done to the black ones the previous day. As soon as the Oxy had dried, he set about his task of doing three more samples of 500 spins each. He had finished by early evening and the results were a carbon copy of the previous day, with red numbers coming out at a rate of 69 per cent for the entire 1,500 rolls.

He had already fixed in his mind what he wanted to do with the coup. He would play the red numbers for £200 per spin for precisely six hours. Any more than that would cause alarm and the casino might start to investigate if money was being lost. They could think that the wheel was biased, which it would be, but not for the reason that they would have originally thought.

The Oxy wouldn't be able to withstand very close scrutiny. Matthew knew this and was the reason why the evidence had to be removed once the coup was completed. Matthew tried to estimate how much he would be ahead betting £200 per spin on red for six hours straight. He figured that an average croupier would spin the ball about thirty times an hour; any more than this would be a bonus.

This meant that he would get 180 spins in the space of six hours. If he could replicate the success on the casino wheel that he had with his own, he would be looking at around 70 per cent of the spins being red numbers. This equated to 126 winning spins, which totalled £25,200. But there would be the other 30 per cent of spins, which totalled fifty-four, where it would either be a losing bet entirely or zero came up, in which case he would get half his bet back.

Matthew calculated the worst case scenario, where all those fifty-four spins were black and this came to a total of £10,800 in losses. This left him with a healthy profit of over fourteen grand. Not a life-changing sum of money, but then again, if it was, the casino would be onto him. He then had the idea of making cover bets on a second roulette table, which would contribute greatly to throwing the casino management off the scent.

He would be placing bets on a second wheel that had no bias and therefore he was subjected to the 1.37 per cent house edge that was against him. He worked out that if he only placed several cover bets per hour on a second table and was prepared to maybe give back a couple of grand by way of disguise, the casino would be highly unlikely to ever find out.

Then he would have to pay Duncan 50 per cent, which would reduce his share to about £6,000, a figure that was based on getting about thirty spins per hour. If the game was relatively quiet or there was a fast dealer on, this figure could be half as much again. The question was whether six grand was enough to warrant taking the risk or whether it would be enough to interest Duncan and tempt him into getting involved.

After all, Duncan would have to get access to the office, fix the camera and apply the Oxy, and it would be he who would be suspected if ever the heat came down. But even small casinos were being hit for five figure sums daily, so what they stood to win wouldn't be looked at too closely, Duncan had already assured him of this. Speaking of Duncan, it was time to make that telephone call.

Give Me a Few Days

When Matthew informed Duncan about the results of the tests, he found them very interesting, but – given Matthew's record of ingenuity – hardly surprising. Now was the moment of truth. Matthew hit Duncan with the big question, "Are we up for it?" He knew that Duncan could do with the money and this may just be the deciding factor in whether or not he said yes. Duncan insisted on seeing a demonstration for himself and they arranged for him to come over to Matthew's house the following evening.

It took about three hours of spinning for Duncan to be convinced that what they had would work in a real environment.

"How do you know that the Oxy will be as invisible on their wheels and also how do you know that it will have the same effect? It may not be the same metal?"

Matthew was quickly trying to ascertain whether Duncan was interested and that this was the reason for his questions, or whether he was just throwing obstacles at Matthew because he didn't want to do it. He quickly figured that Duncan had serious reservations and that if he were to stall with his answers it would only serve to frighten Duncan into not participating in the scam.

"Every roulette wheel manufacturer uses the exact same components in their wheels because of the overwhelming need for randomness. The only difference is in the different types of wood that they use for the bowl, but that doesn't matter to us," replied Matthew. This was bullshit and Matthew knew it, but he wasn't afraid to lie to his best mate; he had done it numerous times before. To people like Matthew, lying just came natural.

"Is that true?"

"You bet," said Matthew, looking Duncan fully in the eye,

which he always did whenever he was lying to someone. He felt it made him more believable.

"I don't know, Matt. Give me a few days to think about it. It's my job you know. If I get caught I could get sent to prison."

"Trust me, that's one thing that won't happen. Sure you'll lose your job and never get another job inside a casino again but you won't get sent to prison. Tampering with wheels is something that has been done countless times before and suspended sentences is all that they get. At the end of the day, they have to prove that we are working as a team and they can't do that. Think about it, if you get caught in the act then all they can do you for is tampering with a wheel. All you do is then contact me and I don't bother to come in and play," replied Matthew, once again thinking very rapidly on his feet.

This was true, but the part about Duncan not being sent to prison and suspended sentences was more bullshit, as Matthew didn't know either way what would happen. Duncan sat there in total silence and Matthew didn't interrupt that silence as he didn't want to appear too pushy, as this would definitely risk losing him. After a few moments Matthew broke the silence: "Hell, Duncan, you are thinking of leaving anyway."

Once again Duncan just sat there in total silence before repeating that he would like time to think it through. They parted company and Matthew told Duncan to have a serious think about it over the next few days.

Let's Rock and Roll

Duncan left it about forty-eight hours before he finally made his mind up about what to do with Matthew's scamming move. It had occupied his every waking thought over the past couple of days but now his mind was made up. It wasn't a life-changing sum of money, but this made it all the more effective. He could pick and choose his moment based on who the afternoon pit boss and duty manager were. There was one pit boss who never checked anything and just went through the motions and one of the female managers would be on her own on a couple of afternoon shifts a week, and she seemed to be a lot weaker than the other managers.

Duncan knew that the rotas for the managers and pit bosses was displayed clearly inside the office, a place to which he had frequent access. He knew from memory that Thursday afternoon was the first day that coincided with these two people working and this was only two days away. As long as Matthew could make Thursday as well, it was shaping up that they could carry out the coup a lot sooner than either of them had dared anticipate.

He telephoned Matthew with the news: "OK mate... let's rock and roll." He explained to Matthew about the slack pit boss and the weak manager and that the first available window was only two days away. This was good in a way because it didn't give Duncan any time to be nervous. He had already attained two replacement security seals in order to reseal the wheel after he had applied the resin. He had managed to do this straightaway as he not only knew where they were kept but that they were not locked away.

There were loads of spare security seals inside the pit desk. He knew, as he had been in the pit area numerous times and seen where they were kept. He had also witnessed numerous times that the desk was closed but not locked, as the afternoon pit boss frequently opened the door without unlocking it. This was it, he was going to do it, but then he thought of something critical that both of them had overlooked.

The manager and pit boss would be different the following

day when he had to go back in and remove the Oxy with the petrol. He knew who the manager and pit boss were on Friday afternoon and he knew from past experience that they were sticklers for detail and security. This very conscientious pit boss would spot the different numbers on the seals, he was sure about that. He called Matthew back immediately and told him what he had just thought of and the potential problem.

"Shit, that's a problem."

"I can't see anyway around it at all."

"Wait a minute," said Matthew, "what if we left the resin in the wheel until these people were working again and then went back to remove it?"

"They are working together again on Sunday afternoon, but that means leaving the Oxy in the wheel for three whole days. Don't you think that this could be stretching it a bit? What if someone notices the number of reds that are coming out and alerts someone? They could easily make the connection between what you did on the Thursday and the abundance of reds. You know full well that this stuff won't stand up to close scrutiny," said Duncan.

"I was going to place some bets on red on another table anyway, to alleviate any possible suspicion of always playing on the same table."

"Will that be enough?"

"Oh I think so," replied Matthew, trying to sound confident, so as not to cause Duncan any more anxiety.

"Three days is an awful long time to leave evidence lying around," repeated Duncan.

"You worry too much, this is nailed on," said Matthew, grinning in the rather cheeky way that he always did. "If we go on

Thursday, can you get the key before then?"

"Oh that's not a problem, I could get it tomorrow."

By Wednesday evening, everything was set. Duncan had the spare wheel seals as well as a replica office key. He even had a small petrol can hidden along with the Oxy inside his sports holdall just in case anything went wrong and he had to remove the evidence quickly.

With his heart thumping like an express train, Duncan set to work with the Oxy on Thursday morning at approximately 6:15am. Every member of staff had vacated the building by 5:30am. First Duncan arranged camera number 6 so that it stayed filming an area of the pit that didn't cover the roulette wheel in question. He continued with his task; the entire operation from entering the pit to adjusting the cameras and then removing the wheel cover and applying the resin took precisely twelve minutes. Having put everything back in place and reset the cameras, he retired to reception and waited for the morning cleaners to arrive, a job very well done.

Into The Valley Of Death

As soon as Duncan arrived home, he contacted Matthew to inform him that everything was in place. Matthew then told Duncan that it would be a very close friend of Matthew's who would come in and do the betting for them. He said to Duncan that he had been having reservations about doing the betting himself because he had already been inside that casino several times. Matthew calculated that if he were to bet as high as £200 per spin his significantly different behaviour would stand out, so it would be better if someone with whom the casino was not familiar did the betting. It was also concerning Matthew that they might find the connection between him and Duncan and this would certainly set the alarm bells ringing.

Duncan listened to Matthew and was forced to agree with everything that he said. "Can we trust this guy?"

"100 per cent. I wouldn't have asked him otherwise."

"So how much are we paying him then?" inquired Duncan.

"5 per cent of whatever we win. At half each, we can live with this," replied Matthew.

"So long as he is honest about how much he is ahead by."

"I would rather have done it myself, Duncan, if I wasn't 100 per cent sure that we could trust him implicitly."

"Fair enough, if you say so."

Duncan wasn't due in for work until around 8:30pm. Matthew had already told Duncan that their accomplice – whose name Matthew had neglected to mention – was going to be using an act as a big hitter. He was told to dress and talk the part and Matthew even gave him his gold Rolex to wear.

Matthew wouldn't be able to let Duncan know during the day just how their man was doing, because he would be out of reach in the pit and mobile phones were still in their infancy back in 1991. But as Duncan was driving to work for his night shift, he was thinking that if anything had gone wrong then surely this guy would have left the casino if he was being wiped out or couldn't get in front. The mere fact that he was told to arrive and play at around 4pm and there had been no word from Matthew by 8pm had to mean that things must have been going well.

He couldn't see the pit from reception and he forced himself to wait until he had a valid reason to go to the office to take a peek across on American Roulette 4. At ten past nine, he had thought of a reason but a feeling of horror went through him as he saw only one punter on AR4, and that punter didn't have any chips on the table. Duncan's heart sank. Was this Matthew's accomplice and if it was, where was the money? Had it all gone horribly wrong? He was dying to know what was happening.

He walked into the office, where the general manager was sitting at his desk. He happened to be looking at the game on AR4 through the camera. "Good evening, John."

"Oh hello," replied John. Duncan could see that the table that he was observing was indeed the table with the gaffed wheel, but he was dying to know what was happening.

"What's the matter, John, you looked lost in thought?"

"Oh it's nothing, Duncan. I'm just watching this lucky bugger on AR4 that's all. He is up about ten grand at the last check and all he's doing is betting on red, the lucky bastard." An unbelievable rush of adrenalin flowed through Duncan's body and he tried desperately hard not to leap up and down screaming and shouting.

"Not to worry, John, you always get it back you know that."

"This will take some getting back, I can tell you. Looks like the entire day's result is shot to pieces at this rate," said John solemnly.

Duncan calmly left the office and took his place back on reception. A short while later, their accomplice – who Duncan learned was called Geoff Maxfield – left the building and never returned. Duncan dared not ask anyone how much this guy had won. No sooner had he arrived home, he telephoned Matthew at 5:45am. He was surprised to find that Matthew answered the telephone almost immediately.

"I knew you wouldn't be able to wait," laughed Matthew out loud. Before Duncan had a chance to respond, Matthew told him that Geoff had finished the session exactly £9,800 in front. This was less than what Matthew had predicted, but it was still a tremendous result all the same. This meant that Geoff's cut would be precisely £490, not bad for six hours' work. This left £9,310 to split between them, coming to just over four and a half grand each.

"Geoff came straight round here after he left the casino, and I already have your money whenever you want to come round and get it. Very good job you did by the way," said Matthew.

"John, the General Manager, was watching the game very intently when I went into the office."

"I expected that he would be. Was anything said?"

"About what?"

"You know, about anything not being quite right."

"Not to my knowledge, they all seemed to think that he was just very lucky, that's all, though I can't vouch for what may have been said in the office. Was Geoff aware of exactly why he was betting on red, have you told him?"

"No. All he knew was that there was a strong bias on the red numbers on that table and to bet on them. He knows nothing about what you did, I promise you."

"Listen, Matt, does Geoff know that he isn't to go back to the casino under any circumstances and repeat what he did last night? If he gets greedy and goes back with his own money, it could rumble us."

"No, he doesn't know the details of the operation but I told him at the outset that the bias would only be temporary. Don't worry, because I had already thought of that."

"Why do you think that we got less than what you predicted?"

"Who knows, but I know one thing and that is that I'm over the moon with the result. I just wish that we didn't have to wait until Sunday to remove the evidence," said Matthew.

"Yeah I know, but listen, Matthew, couldn't we just hit them one more time, maybe on Saturday if the coast is clear? We don't have to hit them to the same level, do we, and you could always go in yourself and instead of betting two hundred quid, maybe no more than fifty?"

"You have to ask yourself if another couple of grand each is worth getting caught. It's possible that they already suspect something and are just waiting for us to be foolish enough to walk back in. Just because they haven't said anything to you, Duncan, doesn't mean that they don't suspect something. No, I say the way to beat these people is to be in and out and leave no pattern and not to get greedy," replied Matthew.

"Maybe you are right."

"I always am, you know that Duncan."

With that the two of them agreed not to repeat the coup for the foreseeable future. Geoff never went back in and did precisely what he was told. Duncan successfully went back and removed the Oxy on Sunday, though he was far more nervous the second time than he was the first. Matthew was right, he thought, they could have suspected something and laid a trap for him. But Sunday came and went and with it the evidence.

The money that they scammed wasn't enough to hurt the casino, nor was it enough to make them rich, but that's entirely the point with these things. It is quite possible that they could have repeated the coup many times over and ended up taking a very substantial amount of money, but the discipline to end the proceedings there and then was very strong with Matthew. It's always the big coups that get noticed and end up on the news and in the newspapers, but it is greed that gets these people caught. It's no good taking a quarter of a million but then getting caught and not only having to pay the money back but also ending up in prison for your troubles.

Chapter 12

The Million Dollar Man

Conspiracy theories abound in many fields and we all love mysteries and stories of shady underworld characters who no one ever gets to meet – those who seemingly control everything and make millions in the process. Whether these people exist in organised crime, the stock market, politics or whatever, we are guilty of sometimes thinking and believing that our fate and destiny is guided by a handful of very powerful and extremely clandestine characters.

The gambling world is certainly no different. The world of horse racing is awash with stories of big betting coups with certain "in the know" punters who have the inside knowledge to hit the bookmakers very hard indeed. But gambling establishments of whatever capacity are fair game and there to be shot at for the handful of people who are shrewd enough to hit them where they are at their weakest.

Only a fool takes on a multi-million pound organisation that has unparalleled expertise at its disposal in the deluded belief that they can get the better of it by attacking it where it is at its strongest. But whether it is the bookmakers, casino owners or whatever, all of them have strengths and they all undoubtedly have weaknesses. The small-time shrewd punters who hit them never get noticed as their winnings are swallowed up by the sea of money that's lost by losing punters.

But sometimes – whether in horse racing, sports betting or casinos – there is an individual who has an aspiration to hit the gambling organisations not just for a few thousand but for tens of millions. The name Vladimir Granec is one that few people who read this book will ever have heard of, which isn't surprising. First, because the events that I'm talking about happened from the mid-1970s to the mid-1980s; second, because once again most of the story was swept under the carpet. In fact many people within the gaming industry itself will not have heard of Vladimir Granec. But in and around 1975, many casinos across the world experienced big losses on roulette and several casinos were hit so severely that they failed to make their yearly targets.

The European gaming police and even the police forces from many different countries were brought in as casino bosses were suspecting a sting on a potentially massive scale. But despite the fact that the gaming industry was receiving substantial help from these authorities, they had no evidence and were reacting through suspicion and nothing else. They had no idea what was happening or indeed who was behind it but they knew that something was not quite right.

But it was the sheer size of Granec's organisation that enabled him to remain anonymous and successful for so long. The casino industry has long since been aware of biased wheels and they were beginning to suspect that they could be on the receiving end of a massive biased-wheel operation of some description. But there are biased wheels and biased wheels. There is a massive difference between the genuine biased wheels exploited by the likes of Billy Walters and Rashid Khan and those that have become biased because of interference from the outside.

Casinos in France, in particular, were especially hit leading to roulette wheels all over the country being carefully removed and examined for bias... Nothing whatsoever was found. But there was soon to be a very significant turn of events, which would lead to almost undeniable proof that something sinister was afoot. A motion detector situated inside a London casino was triggered one early morning after the casino had closed to the public. The motion detector triggered the camera, which amazingly filmed a group of individuals tampering with a roulette wheel.

This was the breakthrough that the authorities had been searching for and when the wheel was inspected a bias was found, which had not been there before, and the cause of the bias was also detected. It is assumed, although it can't be proven, that this group of individuals had somehow hidden inside the casino somewhere before closing time and then came out of their hiding place after everyone had gone home.

But for these individuals to know beyond doubt that there wouldn't be one single person present inside that building from gaming staff to casino managers to security staff defies belief. This seems to indicate once again the distinct possibility of an inside assist in my book. It didn't take long for the suspects to be caught and questioned by the police, and in those interviews one name kept on cropping up: Vladimir Granec.

Granec was Czechoslovakian by birth but lived in Germany. He owned casinos in England and other countries throughout Europe. Further questioning revealed an operation that was highly professional and disciplined and was being planned down to the last detail – and the mastermind appeared to be Vladimir Granec.

After shadowing Granec for some considerable time, the police finally raided his home in Germany. What they found confirmed their suspicions: various bits and pieces of roulette equipment and detailed notes of biased wheels in casinos all over the world. Granec's explanation was that the roulette equipment was inside his house for valid reasons because he owned several casinos – an explanation that hardly holds any water as I'm sure that Donald Trump's house is hardly brimming with roulette wheels and spare parts.

The police obviously didn't believe his story and arrested him, but were forced to let him go for lack of evidence. Despite letting their man get away, the police were not to be put off and arrested Granec again about two years later, but the result was the same: Granec walked because of a lack of evidence.

What exactly were the police aware of and what exactly was Vladimir Granec doing? It seems certain now that the big clue about what was going on was the incident in the London casino, which was caught on camera. The mere thought that one individual could be responsible for getting people on the inside and hitting casinos all over the world for millions is absolutely incredible. But the authorities didn't see it that way and persisted in going after Granec, who was eventually jailed for five years and fined in the region of half a million dollars for his crimes.

Granec had a very successful and highly professional team at his disposal, who were gaining access to casinos after they had closed and then creating some sort of bias within the roulette wheels. They selected the casinos that had the weakest security systems and the most accessible places for Granec's associates to hide. Once the team had fixed the wheels a big betting accomplice would go in and the rest as they say is history. The question of how much Granec's organisation make in total can't easily be answered. I've read numerous figures and reports on the subject and the sum of $10 million is a commonly accepted figure, but I think it is pitifully low.

If the authorities estimated that Granec had made $10 million based on the evidence they had, how much had he made if one took into account all the incidents that they couldn't prove? And who is to say that Granec wasn't secretly masterminding coups long after his "retirement"? It seems obvious to me that knowledge like this doesn't stay dormant for long and tends to get reused or passed on to others. Granec had a desire to hit the gaming industry and this desire never goes away – I can speak from personal experience. If Granec and his team hadn't made at least double the figure of $10 million I would be very surprised.

It seems feasible to me that Granec and his team could have made as much as $50 million. This guy was the real Mr Big of roulette and the undisputed Godfather. But what this case proves beyond any shadow of a doubt is that the casinos can be got at by anyone who has the drive and resources – not to mention the intelligence – to do it.

Vladimir Granec deserves to be at the very front of this book and not at the back, and should definitely be in my hall of fame. But I wanted to award him the honour of giving him a chapter all by himself because of his formidable achievement. Yes I know that deliberately fixing roulette wheels is a criminal offence and this makes Granec a criminal. Yes I know that I shouldn't be singing the praises of known criminals, but you can't help but admire a man with that much determination and guile.

Granec was a man after my own heart and I'm sure that had I ever had the chance to meet him we would have had a lot in common. Granec hit the casinos just like I had done, but many times greater. He was in a league all by himself and I have no shame whatsoever in bowing to the King.

CONCLUSION

In this book we have delved into the past and looked at the early roulette pioneers like Joseph Jaggers and William Darnborough. We have also looked at more recent figures like Rashid Khan and the "Montgomery" brothers. What we have failed to do is to look into the future. One may ask "Is this possible?" and the answer would be "It depends". Will the game of roulette prove to be as vulnerable in the future as it has been in the past?

How many times can the gaming industry be caught with its pants around its ankles? As I conclude this book there is a case going through court in England of a team of Chinese scammers who took about a quarter of a million pounds on three-card poker using hidden cameras up their sleeves. They operated in casinos all over England. What staggered me about this case was that they were rehashing old scams and getting away with it for six figure sums.

You would be mistaken for thinking that the more scams that get revealed, the greater the knowledge would be on behalf of the casinos. Increased knowledge should bring with it increased security and safety, but this is obviously not the case. The fact that a team of scammers can still hit the casinos in this way and get away with it, to a certain extent, just underlines this. If they hadn't been too greedy, they would have been very unlikely to have got caught.

All these people did was to rehash an old trick on a new game in a different era. I refuse to believe that experienced gaming professionals couldn't possibly be aware of this move. This leaves just one possible explanation – the casinos were once again made vulnerable by complacent staff. This is the silent killer, always has been and always will be. The headline in the newspaper that ran the article about this team called it "James Bond style spy equipment" as though the likes of it had never been seen or heard of before.

But using cameras, computers and other equipment to get an edge over casinos has all been done before. It's just that as the technology gets better and smaller it makes it easier to accomplish. In my first blackjack team, we used modern technology to assist us by way of a laptop computer with a shuffle-tracking computer program installed on it. We also experimented with cellular phones that vibrated silently to secretly signal in big betting blackjack players. There are no boundaries to imagination and creativity, and no defence either.

In the new, high-tech age of gaming and roulette, a lot of the older moves become obsolete. As it becomes the norm in computerised roulette for punters to use computer touch screens to make their bets, while a single croupier spins the ball on a single centralised wheel, much of the conventional game is rapidly disappearing. But if you think that this will bring an end to scamming and advantage play, you couldn't be more wrong. All it will do is attract a much more sophisticated and technologically minded cheat and advantage player.

There is a constantly repeating pattern of events where the gaming industry continues in peaceful bliss and ignorance in the belief that it is safe, until something happens to remind them that there are people who are out to get them. As long as they are winning and meeting their targets they are happy. In fact this is precisely the time to hit a casino, when the management and owners are happy. I know from personal experience that when a casino happens to be experiencing a losing period it is precisely the time when managers and pit bosses start to assess and look at things, and security generally tightens up.

That guy who won five grand last week will be looked at a lot more closely than if he had won the money during a period of good results for the casino. What this proves once again is how vulnerable casinos feel, especially on games with high pay-offs like roulette and Caribbean stud poker. Both of them are bad games if you are playing them on the level but odds of 35 to 1 on roulette and as high as 50 to 1 on Caribbean stud poker make the games a magnet for the cheats. So the upshot of all this is that casinos are as vulnerable today as they have always been and anyone with enough creativity or a large dose of guts and determination can get at them and take them for very substantial amounts of money.

The case of the Chinese scammers on three-card poker is only the latest episode in a story that's as long as the gaming industry itself. The only things that change are the amounts, the people and the locations. But anything that's invented by man can be overcome by man. Irrespective of how much knowledge and security systems there are available to a casino, they will forever be second best to the cheat with one outstanding asset in their arsenal… imagination!

Poker books from D&B